THE AGILE
MARKETER

THE AGILE MARKETER

TURNING CUSTOMER EXPERIENCE INTO YOUR COMPETITIVE ADVANTAGE

ROLAND SMART

WILEY

Published by John Wiley & Sons, Inc., Hoboken, New Jersey
Published simultaneously in Canada

Library of Congress Cataloging-in-Publication Data is on File:

9781119223009 (hbk)
9781119223016 (ePDF)
9781119223030 (epub)

Cover Design: Wiley
Cover Image: Roland Smart

Printed in the United States of America

10 9 8 7 6 5 4 3 2 1

Contents

strategy and UX to communications. Learn how Agile practices are increasingly becoming a platform for engagement between all facets of product management and marketing.

Who owns innovation? The practice of innovation is broader than Agile practice and represents an opportunity for marketing and product management to collaborate. Two exercises provide a framework for defining which groups "own" the inputs to the innovation process.

Who owns the customer experience? Different groups may own different parts of the customer experience, but marketers are uniquely positioned to map and measure it. Learn how marketing driven research programs and psychology provide insights into opportunities that would be overlooked from a purely Agile perspective.

How does the customer relationship change as companies modernize their marketing function? When customers help design the product, more opportunities arise for them to advocate for it. (Incidentally, they are ultimately advocating for your culture as much as they are for your product or service.)

What if the product was also the marketing? A case study illustrates how the freemium model is both a product and a marketing service. Also, how to leverage gamification to support the marketing of your products.

Can your community also be your competitive advantage? More and more companies are using the crowd to disrupt markets, and marketplace-based business models are disrupting many industries. The so-called collaborative economy, in which both customers as well as external providers actively shape the product (or service), is now passing an inflection point. Established businesses must consider either how to become "crowd companies" or adopt crowd practices to advance their products and services.

Preface

The goal of this book is to share some of what I've learned from my own journey as a marketer. My motivation stems from the fact that some of my greatest insights have come from books that I've read while learning my trade in the trenches. Books like *Competitive Advantage*, *Innovation and Entrepreneurship*, *The Cluetrain Manifesto*, *The Innovator's Dilemma*, *Crossing the Chasm*, *Predictably Irrational*, *The Lean Startup*, and *Digital Body Language*—to name a few—made me stop and reevaluate how to approach my work. Sometimes they even took me in a completely new direction that proved rewarding. I've applied the insights from these readings over the years in ventures that succeeded and ventures that failed. Throughout my journey, I've been exposed to just about every aspect of marketing. I've also been fortunate to work at companies where I could balance my interest in marketing and product design with my broader interest in entrepreneurialism and business. This explains why I've grown to be a product-oriented marketer who appreciates and embraces contemporary innovation practices.

My interest in marketing technology started in earnest when I joined a consumer packaged goods company as its first employee. Adina was founded and managed by a successful entrepreneur, Greg Steltenpohl, whose previous company, Odwalla, was acquired by The Coca-Cola Company. For three years, I worked with him running the marketing group. We launched three products into national distribution as social marketing became a thing.

After moving to the San Francisco Bay Area to join Adina full time, I quickly became immersed in the marketing technology community. I joined a remarkable user experience (UX) design firm named Adaptive Path (which has since been acquired by Capital One). Adaptive Path was working on some of the most cutting-edge social technologies on behalf of such clients as Flickr, MySpace, and Nokia. Though Adaptive Path specialized in UX design, I probably learned more about marketing there than at any other place I've worked. That's because the company was laser-focused on improving the process by which companies develop products and services with customer experience in mind. Though I did not know this at the time, these same approaches would ultimately transform my view of marketing.

Later I joined Sprout, the first of two marketing technology start-ups where I would be responsible for leading the marketing group. Sprout was acquired by InMobi, at the time the largest independent mobile advertising network. The second company, Involver, was acquired by Oracle, where I am currently the VP of Social and Community Marketing.

Much of my work today centers on the Oracle Technology Network, but I am also part of a cohort of marketers who are focused on modernizing Oracle's own marketing platform with many of the scores of technologies we have acquired, including Eloqua, Responsys, BlueKai, Compendium, Vitrue, and Involver.

It's in this capacity that I've been exposed to the enormity of the challenge that marketers face today. The marketing technology industry is going through a tremendous cycle of innovation. New technologies have yielded unprecedented business value based on deeper insights into customer behavior, but the speed and volume of innovation has also spawned new problems: data fragmentation, platform/product overlap and integration overhead, as well as challenges to management structures and traditional organizational norms.

My hope is that this book will help you overcome some of these challenges in your efforts to modernize your marketing practices and the platforms that support them. Part 1 explains why and how the adaptive development approaches used by development organizations are driving change in the marketer's world. Part 2 examines these approaches in detail and how they work in a marketing context. In Part 3, we explore how adaptive approaches can be integrated with traditional marketing practices, how they change relationships across the C-suite, and how they ultimately lead to better internal alignment. Finally, Part 4 focuses on what modern marketing looks like in practice, how it changes the relationship between the company and its community of customers, and how it uniquely positions marketers as the steward of customer experience.

In short, *The Agile Marketer* presents ideas to help marketers create a new culture to meet the imperatives of modern marketing. Let me emphasize up front that this book is not intended to be a comprehensive guide to implementation. Such a book would be nearly impossible to write, given how company-specific the cultural transformation that implementation requires must be. But herein you will find numerous examples of the kinds of strategies and tactics that you'd expect to implement as part of a transformation, regardless of your industry, the nature of your organization, or the maturity of your current marketing practice. I hope these ideas help make your journey productive and successful.

Roland Smart
September 2015

Acknowledgments

Many marketers provided feedback on this book during its development. For the last year it has been evolving as a shared document with more than 25 collaborators logging in to comment, suggest changes, and make edits. In this way, it's fair to say the book has been developed using an Agile process.

Oracle deserves recognition for its support of this project and for making internal teams and customers available to participate. Beyond this access, my colleagues at Oracle have inspired me—and challenged me—to expand my thinking about how to apply an approach that was pioneered at smaller companies inside the enterprise. Their willingness to grapple with these ideas, provide feedback, and share insights has demonstrably improved this book.

I also had the great fortune of working with a talented editor, Jan Koch, whose efforts went well beyond editing.

Finally, a heartfelt thanks to my wife, Alicia Smart, for her support and encouragement throughout this project.

THE AGILE MARKETER

How
Development
Methods
Influence
Marketing

1

Why Marketing Needs to Adapt

Why do marketers need a new approach?

With the rise of social media, marketers entered an era of heightened exposure in which any kind of product or brand failure has the potential to echo virally and at lightning speed through the marketplace. This vulnerability has intensified the pressure on companies to treat customers better and to share information with them in a more transparent manner. And the information sharing has evolved to include the active solicitation of feedback to incorporate at increasingly earlier stages of the product cycle. Many refer to this period as the "age of the empowered customer." In this book I'll explain how it's also poised to be an "age of the marketer."

This heightened exposure has certainly benefited the customer, but it has also benefited those companies that have organized themselves to harness customer feedback to quickly improve their products and services. Those companies that can meet and exceed customer expectations (that is, create a great customer experience) have a competitive advantage. Because marketers play a critical role as a conduit between the customer and the company, they are positioned to have a greater role in the business than ever before. In fact, if they get it right, they have an opportunity to serve as the steward of the overall customer experience.

Many marketers are starting to recognize this possibility. But few would claim to be close to achieving this stewardship role. The truth is, there are far more companies that don't get it right. If anything, they are undermining the customer experience. But let's consider for a moment what kinds of customer experiences trigger criticism and harsh responses. No doubt some of these examples will ring a bell for you:

- The company whose software you use to organize your photos does a major relaunch of its site with no warning, and suddenly you can't find all of your photos. You visit their community to find that many users are having the same issue, but no one seems to have a definitive answer on how the new system works.
- You buy a product from the manufacturer, only to have one of its retailers offer you the same product at a discount a week later. You e-mail customer support; they are unaware of the promotion and unwilling to offer you a refund.
- You reach out for customer support on Twitter, go through the process of mutual "following" so that you can direct-message and then explain the issue, only to get redirected to another channel where you have to start all over again.
- You research a product online and find some great reviews, but you've also spotted some dismal ones, and the company has not responded to the concerns. You reach out on social media to hear from the company, but they don't respond.
- You visit an online clothing retailer and browse its entire sweater catalog. The company follows up with a series of e-mails containing offers, but none are for sweaters. You then pass by one of the company's retail stores on your way to work and discover that there was a storewide sale over the weekend.
- You call one of your phone service provider's retail locations to ask if it does handset exchanges in-store. The representative says "yes" and tells you to come over, but when you arrive you discover there's an hour wait for service. The clerk asks for your phone number but then tells you that you have to stay in the store in order to keep your appointment. When your turn finally comes up, the clerk informs you that in-store exchanges are subject to a restocking fee that does not apply to online exchanges.

Every one of these examples is the result of a failure that is due—at least in part—to marketing platforms and practices that have not kept pace with innovation and customer expectations. They represent a disconnect between marketing and the group responsible for developing the product or service. None of these, moreover, is a small failure, because even a single poor customer experience can do long-lasting harm to the company's reputation (especially if you haven't delivered a particularly great experience in the same period). What's more, within every one of these examples there are many opportunities for the company to deliver a consistent and great experience that could differentiate it and establish loyalty.

These are hardly isolated examples. Many companies suffer from these same flaws. Comcast is frequently held up as a poster child for customer complaints—complaints over customer service, billing practices, and the customer experience on its websites. In fact, so long is the list of complaints that there's even a Twitter hashtag—#comcastoutrage—where the disgruntled can vent. At the heart of the complaints is frustration over Comcast's approach to its core service: The company forces customers to buy services in bundles that include many items that they simply don't want. Granted this can be an effective way to get customers to try new content, but Comcast has taken it to such an extreme that it actually infuriates customers.

The fact is that Comcast's approach has for years been out of sync with the market's direction. And that is why services like HBO diversified and joined forces with younger Comcast competitors that are allowing customers to buy just what they want, when they want it.

An empowered marketing organization that was aligned with the rest of the company would have early on recognized this as a problem with the marketing mix (in this case, the mix of products and prices). It would have engaged with the core service team to address it. In companies where marketing is disconnected, marketing is relegated to amplifying the success of good products—which often don't need much help—or doing damage control by spinning the facts in the best possible light (if the product is bad). Either represents a reactive, if not impoverished, approach to marketing from which the stewardship of customer experience is out of reach.

To put this in perspective, consider that just 30 years ago, we were still living in the so-called broadcast era of marketing, when brand perception could be managed quite effectively by marketers. Then, innovation was often driven by marketing, and product development had less influence; it was there to execute. Companies could get away with this approach because consumers had little ability to share their experiences freely or amplify their voices above the companies' megaphones. So companies faced less pressure to improve their products and services. On top of this, the broadcast system constituted an ecosystem that favored a smaller number of bigger brands competing for attention.

What's remarkable is how quickly things changed. Greater access to affordable development tools, combined with the rise of social media, drove the pendulum to the opposite extreme. It happened with such force that at the most innovative companies innovation is now more often driven by product management. The problem now is that companies have gotten so good at innovating quickly that they can readily replicate each other's products and services. What they cannot replicate as easily, however, is a consistent and great customer experience. This fact is what's driving the pendulum back toward the middle where the group managing the product or service development and the marketing group need to collaborate closely in order to compete effectively in the marketplace.

Companies like Comcast are sitting on top of an enormous opportunity, though, because they have relationships with the majority of customers in their market spaces. And those customers have feedback and ideas that Comcast could transform into value—if Comcast could only overcome its unbalanced approach to product development and marketing. Indeed, it's got a lot of work to do: Millennials do not see Comcast as the innovative content-delivery platform that it once was. Rather, they are apt to think of Comcast as an entrenched company that lobbies the government to maintain unfair (i.e., monopolistic) access to the market.

The fact is that Comcast has enjoyed a de facto monopoly for a long time, and that has insulated it from the need to treat customers well. It's as if the company is still operating in the broadcast era. Comcast may be profiting from this insulation, but in the process, those functions that would make it competitive in a nonmonopolistic market have atrophied. To thrive in the future, Comcast will have to undergo a major transformation in order to compete with the wealth of innovative alternatives now available on the content distribution side of their business—never mind facing off against the new entrants whose aim to establish alternatives to landline-based Internet connections would threaten Comcast's monopolistic access to customers.

In fairness, Comcast seems to be recognizing these challenges; the company has already appointed new management with a stated goal of focusing on customer experience. And it is making progress. Managing a turnaround will not be easy, but it is possible if the company embraces a new approach to both innovation (new service development) and marketing that is balanced and collaborative. This book is about that new approach and how it aligns product and service development with marketing. This approach is designed to help companies like Comcast understand their customers better, harness their feedback, and design for customers' evolving needs. It's not a new multiyear strategic plan, rather it's an approach that delivers one small victory after another in a battle to stay relevant.

What Does Modern Marketing Feel Like Today?

Modern marketing is fundamentally about competing on the basis of the customer experience. Doing so effectively requires new practices and platforms; throughout this book, I map out the path to modernizing marketing. My intention in using this term is to underscore a company's ability to compete on the basis of customer experience.

To get a sense of the direction marketing is taking, consider this hypothetical example, based on a real product and its real issues. You're a successful millennial with a top job at a growing company based in a major metropolitan area. You're in the market for a new car, but you harbor mixed feelings about new cars because they're hard on the environment. So you've decided on an electric car, which reflects your environmentally conscious values. You're hoping you can find one that will also send a message about your accomplishments (not to mention satisfying your ego's need for speed).

This may well be your single biggest purchase to date. As you are inclined to do, you'll start your search by browsing on your mobile device and asking for suggestions on social.

Facebook picks up your intentions and presents an ad for a hybrid Cadillac. You knowingly take the bait and investigate its site. You also download the Cadillac's mobile app before heading out to the dealership to learn more. Sitting in the car, the first thing you notice is the Cadillac User Experience (CUE) display. You can connect your phone but that doesn't add much value to your experience. That's disappointing. You take the test drive, though, and return to the showroom to briefly get some idea about available options and pricing.

Later that day, you get a notification on your phone pointing to an article about Tesla that a friend is sharing with you on Facebook. You've heard that the car was rated "best new car of the year" by a number of automotive publications and reviewers. The article touts new features coming out in 2015 that will make it impossible for the car to run out of range. It's hard not to worry about range with an electric, so this peaks your interest.

You learn that Tesla updates its cars in the same way that your phone gets updated. In this case, the company released a firmware update that directed drivers to one of its SuperCharger stations when their cars were running low on battery. With your phone in hand, you check out Tesla's mobile app and discover that it lets you check the car's charging progress, preheat or cool the car, locate it, and even access it remotely. You jump to Tesla's website, which lets you schedule a test drive.

There's nothing typical about Tesla's showroom. For one thing, it's in a retail location, nestled between a home furnishing store and a clothing boutique. For another, they're expecting you. There's certainly nothing typical about Tesla's approach to making and selling cars. You learn that Tesla does not release cars on an annual basis like Cadillac. Instead, the company is continuously improving and updating the car's hardware and software; the model you're interested in, for example, will add additional self-driving features with future software releases. Teslas are made to order and offer many configuration choices that you'll want to explore. The entire buying experience is different.

You resist the urge to make a rash decision. Of course, these cars are made to order so you couldn't drive away with one right now even if you wanted to. Plus, you can't ignore the fact that the car costs a good bit more than the Cadillac and much more than you ever imagined spending on a vehicle. But this car doesn't feel like something that starts depreciating as soon as you drive out of the dealership. On the contrary, the car seems like it will improve over time.

Now you need to get a better idea of the car's reputation. What do its owners think? Unlike the Cadillac, Tesla has a community of owners who are actively engaged online. So you start poking around.

You discover that Tesla has had some issues, for example with the battery. The car originally lowered itself at high speeds to improve efficiency. Unfortunately, this feature caused battery damage for some drivers when they ran over objects in the road or hit rough pavement. But Tesla addressed this with a software update that disabled the height adjustment as well as with the installation of new bottom-plate hardware. The company also issued a series of communications to owners about the problem and provided release notes for the software update. Most important, users remained satisfied, undeterred, even; they continue to recommend the car.

A negative piece you came across in the *New York Times* claimed that Tesla's mileage estimates were inaccurate. Elon Musk, Tesla's CEO (and product architect), promptly refuted the story, using data from the car that the journalist drove. He also took the opportunity to point out that Tesla is constantly improving the customer experience based on similar data and input from customers.

Your experience thus far has been great: clear, consistent, and straightforward. Granted, there have been some issues, but that's to be expected from a company that's disrupting an industry. In fact, part of what sets Tesla apart is how it has responded to these issues—which is to say, promptly, factually, and transparently. What you hear on social media aligns with what the company is saying. This is the car you're going to buy.

Driving into the Future

Tesla develops and manufactures its cars using an adaptive approach that makes it possible to innovate quickly and respond to unexpected circumstances that in another era (or with another company) could have derailed a fledgling business. On Tesla's manufacturing side, the approach is called *Lean*; on the software side, it's called *Agile*. Both are adaptive approaches. From a marketer's perspective, what is most impressive is that the automaker's approach to marketing echoes, complements, and enhances its approach to development. It's as if the marketing and the product development are so tightly aligned that they're virtually indistinguishable. With Tesla, this may literally be the case, considering that Elon Musk is as much a product guy as he is a marketer (whether he admits this or not). Marketing and product development can iterate right alongside each other, as they evolve the product and brand ever more closely to the customer's ideal. And, perhaps most importantly, they are in lockstep when it comes to delivering a consistent and great user experience.

In fact, Tesla extended its development approach to marketing, which turns out to be a critical first step on the road to modern marketing. As you'd expect, Tesla established a community early on; it is listening to customers and addressing product concerns in a public way. Such transparency is at the heart of an adaptive approach.

Tesla stands in contrast to Comcast along many dimensions: industry, age, size, and competitive profile. But the most important dimension in which the two companies differ is internal alignment. Comcast is not old in years, but it is in terms of its innovation and marketing practices. Upstart companies with agility—those that can adopt contemporary approaches out of the gate—are driving Comcast's customers to "cut the cord." To maintain its historic growth rate, it must change more than the way it develops new services; it must develop them in lockstep with marketing.

For the marketing group, modernization has major implications for two areas: (1) marketing practices and (2) the platforms and technology that support those practices. Of course, these implications are intertwined and can't be understood independently. What we'll discover, as with Tesla, is that the practices that Comcast needs to adopt are actually derived from those used by product development. Marketing must follow development's example to facilitate this transformation.

The Relationship between Product Development and Marketing

The processes that development organizations employ to develop products or services have, of course, evolved over the years. Traditionally, they started with the business requirements document, which would then go to design. Once designed, the product would get thrown over the fence to development, where it would undergo many stages of revision. Finally, it would be tested for release. Throughout the process, the product would be handled by a handful of separate teams. The product owner, or business lead, might not have checked in on the process until nearly the end of the project.

Over the past 15 years or so, as the pace of innovation has accelerated, and product development cycles have been compressed, this traditional approach has become increasingly impractical. This is because the old way attempts to predict what the end state of the product will be, whereas the new way adapts the product or service direction to customer feedback along the way. Though both approaches include the same steps (e.g., design, development, testing), the predictive approach measures twice and cuts once, whereas the adaptive approach is constantly measuring while making many small cuts.

Agile (the dominant adaptive approach to building software) is optimal for contexts where you can't predict what you'll need to build but where time-to-value is of the essence. Popularized by start-ups that needed to be able to pivot quickly as they zeroed in on the right product/market fit, Agile has become solidly mainstream, implemented at some of the biggest technology companies in the world (including Oracle). It's been critically important for big companies, where a rapid response to market changes is invariably a tougher undertaking.

So what does all this have to do with marketing?

Most marketers have not experienced Agile first hand. This isn't surprising; marketers haven't traditionally cared much about how things worked under the hood, as long as they worked. That was IT's job.

Good marketing has always required having a deep understanding of how the company's products and services are purchased and used. But that's no longer enough. We must also understand how these products and services are *developed*. This is because marketing needs to actively collaborate on the development of products and services. For one thing, the adaptive approaches to development depend on constant feedback from customers to support iteration. Marketers, as the stewards of the brand's community, are perfectly positioned to act as a feedback conduit between the customer and the product development organization. As such, marketers have the potential to play a more effective, more strategic role in facilitating the product/market fit. Indeed, Tesla is attempting just that, albeit in a rudimentary way: The company's community forums call for direct feedback with posts whose subject lines read "TESLA WANTS FEEDBACK ON ANY POOR (OR GREAT!) CUSTOMER EXPERIENCES" (their caps).[1]

There's another reason why marketing needs to understand product development: The technology required to execute modern marketing is a service in its own right. In other words, marketers must act as the product owner as they integrate a range of marketing technologies and build out their platforms. Such platforms will have to deliver consistent and great customer experiences. And that's important because customer experience is quickly becoming the battleground on which companies compete. A recent Gartner survey of marketing leaders found that 89 percent of companies "plan to compete primarily on the basis of the customer experience by 2016." Yet "fewer than half of companies surveyed rate their customer experience as exceptional today."[2] This seems overly optimistic (not to mention somewhat characteristic of self-reported data), although it does support the general trend of viewing the customer experience as the foundation of competitive advantage.

Clearly there's a chasm between the aspiration and the reality. Following traditional approaches, marketers would plan to take a year designing and building a bridge to cross that chasm. But because the marketing technology landscape is so complex and is evolving so rapidly, the far side of the chasm will have moved by the time the marketer gets there. That's why adaptive approaches are so essential. Adopting an adaptive approach has become an imperative for marketers who aspire to become stewards of the customer experience.

2 The Modern Marketer's Challenge

The entrepreneur always searches for change, responds to it, and exploits it as an opportunity.[1]

—Peter Drucker

Marketing leaders today face enormous possibilities—and an enormous challenge. Thanks to the rich troves of data now available to them, they see the opportunity to compete on the basis of personalized customer experiences. But they also inhabit a marketing technology landscape that is complex, fragmented, rapidly evolving—in short, overwhelming. This landscape is replete with overlapping technologies, integration challenges, data fragmentation, and technology management that borders on the labyrinthine. Just search for Scott Brinker's marketing technology landscape infographic to see one person's attempt to bring some order to this dizzyingly complex picture. But be prepared to zoom in deep to this almost comically dense graphic. As helpful as it is, it doesn't at all capture the integration points between the technologies.

What the vast breadth of technologies in this cluttered field tells us is that investors have fully bought into the notion that marketing technology can make better customer experiences possible, and will thus drive competition in the future. Indeed, powerful solutions are emerging, solutions that allow us to understand our customers (and potential customers) like never before. Insights from Big Data make it possible, for instance, for Facebook to know when a user is likely to exit a romantic relationship, in many cases before they actually do.[2] That's an extreme example, to be sure. But the point is that these technologies help us better understand our customers so we can serve them better and build stronger relationships with them. Among these technologies, to name just a handful:

- Web technologies that allow us to track people across the web and to understand browsing behavior.
- Social technologies that let us measure influence and understand who is driving the conversation on specific topics.
- Advertising technologies that enable us to test messaging and understand which messages resonate most with which market segments.
- Retail technologies that let us track how customers navigate our stores and understand what merchandising methods are most effective.
- Business intelligence technologies that allow us to establish correlations between the above data sources.

All such discrete solutions demonstrate that marketers can leverage new technologies to benefit the business overall. But there's a greater need: a complete, integrated marketing platform that combines the discrete benefits of specific technologies into a whole. That whole includes a complete picture of the customer and an apparatus to engage with that individual in a personalized way—and to do so at scale. If we marketers could realize this need, our impact would be profound: multiplicative rather than additive.

By "integrated marketing platform" I do not mean a single interface that marketers can log into to manage all of their marketing programs and data. Rather, I'm referring to a technology stack that includes discrete technologies (such as social listening, ad retargeting, data exchange, influencer management, and community platforms) that are layered on top of foundational technologies (such as customer relationship management, marketing automation, content management, and databases).

The integrated marketing platform is one that includes an established framework for connecting discrete technologies and a consistent approach to data management, aggregation, and intelligence. Such a platform, in turn, supports agility, the ability to innovate, and the ability to scale. Investors (and the biggest technology companies) are already making this vision a reality. They know it's no longer a question of whether, but of when—and of which companies will be the winners.

The Marketing Buyer's Perspective

Mind the modern marketing vision gap. On one side are so-called best-in-class solutions, developed by smaller and more agile firms. These solutions don't suffer from the bloat associated with maturity. This is part of what allows them to compete with solutions from bigger, more mature companies. Their offerings feel more contemporary, easy to use, and focused. On the other side are solutions that promise deep integration between systems, solutions that are only achievable by the biggest tech houses. I'm talking about tight integrations between point-of-sale, customer relationship management, human resources, finance, and marketing systems that don't rely heavily on systems integrators. These solutions come with sophisticated permission models that manage access and address compliance issues that the small firms typically cannot.

In this battle, the big companies have war chests with which to acquire up-and-comers. These acquisitions target the best technologies and the best talent while filling portfolio gaps. If you've been watching the marketing technology landscape in the last couple of years, you could not have missed the breathless pace of acquisitions by the biggest players.

Admittedly this description is a bit of an oversimplification. The fact is that the big guys like Oracle are becoming more agile through a steady diet of acquisitions. And the little guys are getting really smart in building interoperability into their applications. In short, a race to the middle is taking place. Recent history has shown that the majority of top technologies get picked up and absorbed into the portfolios of enterprise players. The biggest tech companies can afford to address the overlap between technologies while also developing deep integrations, although this does take time—time that gives up-and-comers room to innovate and kick off the cycle all over again.

Smart marketers consider this reality as they survey the landscape and contemplate their own marketing platforms. But there are other issues to consider as well, such as how they'll develop and manage their platform. Will they manage the service internally, or will they rely on partners and agencies to support them? Figure 1.1 is a common representation of these decision points and the trade-offs.

The reality, of course, is much more nuanced, because "best-in-class" and "integrated" are not necessarily mutually exclusive. In fact, the below graph

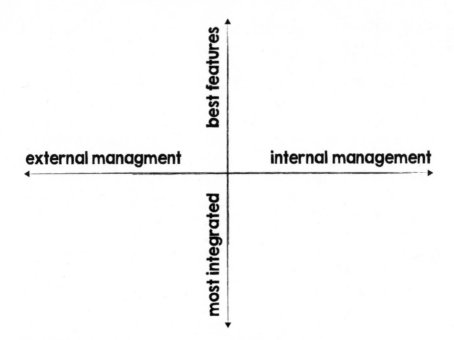

FIGURE 1.1 Misleading Technology Decision Graph

is actually misleading because integration will ultimately be a qualification of what makes a product/service best in class. And the boundary between internal management and external management will be blurred by the fact that every company will be working with hybrid stacks. They'll manage some of the platform and rely on partners for other parts. Some technologies will be managed on-premise and some will be managed in the cloud depending on the degree of customization, security, and integration that is required. So those partners that can support a hybrid stack will be most competitively positioned.

For these reasons, marketing clouds like Oracle's will not require customers to use an Oracle-only stack. Rather, the same integration interfaces that tie into other Oracle solutions will also support third-party solutions. And this capability is being reinforced by smaller acquired companies that have established a broad range of integrations before being acquired. Granted, some integrations may be deprecated for competitive reasons, but arguably this is the exception—and it's rarely a smart strategic move.

One way to tame the complexity associated with this situation is to first focus on the core components of your platform. I subscribe to the view that the foundational technology of any marketing platform should be the database, because data must be aggregated across all systems in order to deliver insights from Big Data. The ground level of the stack is then composed of a customer relationship management platform and the marketing automation platform. These platforms represent the choices that you'll have to live with over the long haul. And, they'll affect the choices you make about the myriad technologies that sit on top of them in your stack. Typically, the cost of changing out the upper layers of the stack is a fraction of what it costs to make foundation-level changes.

Entering the Era of Modern Marketing

Let's return to Tesla, whose marketing programs are today relatively basic. Tesla currently benefits from a first-mover advantage that effectively reduces the pressure on marketing as the principal architect of competitive advantage. With its sustained growth, however, Tesla will need more sophisticated techniques to fully wed product development to marketing as competition inevitably increases. And Tesla needs more competition, as Elon Musk has himself stated publicly, to fully establish the electric car market and its supporting infrastructure. To this end, Musk has even given away Tesla's patents.[3] He knows his approach to innovation and marketing will ensure competitiveness—more than patents will—once the market is fully established.

As a young (and well-funded) company, Tesla can afford to build an integrated marketing platform from scratch. But even for Tesla, the vision of an integrated marketing platform is still only aspirational. Today, Tesla delivers a good and consistent experience across a small number of touchpoints, but the experience during the buyer's journey is not nearly as smart as the experience of driving the car. Can Tesla follow a customer across its website, mobile application, and in-store experience to deliver marketing touches at just the right moment—and dramatically influence what is typically a highly emotional decision? Is it leveraging data from its community to personalize its website? Is it leveraging its most influential advocates effectively? Does the company use technology to understand where its prospects are in the buyer's journey? Can it connect the dots to deliver the right message at the right time via the right channel to the right customer to optimize sales growth? How does the company measure marketing's impact on sales?

An integrated marketing platform is still beyond the reach of most marketers; their hands are already full just trying to optimize existing systems while they also keep an eye on new opportunities arising from technological innovation. When they do find new technologies that might help them innovate and modernize, they often do not have ample discretionary resources to experiment. To make matters worse, they often get caught in a cycle of trying to justify an investment before they can prove what the results will be.

Marketers are so overwhelmingly busy that, like so many leaders, they often struggle to focus beyond the short term. But the shift to modern marketing represents a major change, in practice and in mind-set. Time and resources matter, but it's leadership that's needed most to bridge the chasm between the vision of an integrated marketing platform and the fragmented reality of today.

Faced with a flood of discrete technologies that do not fit together neatly, marketers often feel as if they are on their own. There are no instructions, and they have only incompatible components and glue in hand to build a platform that bridges the aforementioned chasm. In some ways, their situation resembles working at the start of the industrial revolution, when standards and interchangeable parts were a new concept. Marketers cobble together "Franken-platforms" that can deliver amazing results, but that are neither elegant nor flexible, that are hard to upgrade, and that take a long time to deliver value. Worse still, all the technology often becomes a distraction from the fundamental tasks of connecting with customers in a simple, clear and concise fashion.

So figuring out how to get from point A to point B is difficult. Marketers need a new approach, new practices, and technology expertise. Because marketers have established the vision for what's possible with an integrated marketing platform and because they've demonstrated the value of discrete technologies, some have already been able to unlock enough resources to start tackling this new challenge. Indeed, virtually every industry analyst has predicted that marketers are about to spend more on technology than their IT departments. Along with a bigger budget comes greater influence but also greater expectations. Marketing leaders are gazing longingly across the chasm, yet their teams lack experience in converting a pile of technologies into a platform that will get them to the promised land.

Sure, talented people can change the way they work together to overcome obstacles. But it's hard to even take the first step when you're facing a goal so daunting and an obstacle that's far afield of your area of expertise. No doubt (and analysts are predicting this) chief marketing officers (CMOs) will resort to poaching talent from IT. But that alone is not the answer. CMOs cannot operate in competition with CTOs or CIOs. Rather, they must work in partnership with them, with an understanding of shared values and benefits. This is why the CMO/CTO/CIO partnership is so imperative: Beyond having the technology talent, IT also has the process. They're experienced in the adaptive approach. They know how to make Agile (and Lean) work.

And why is it so important to get this partnership right from the start? You need only think of the first generation of IT infrastructure to recall how long-term the consequences of today's technology decisions can be. Establishing an integrated marketing platform takes a significant investment, one that can't, and won't, be revisited in the short term.

Catching Up from Behind

On top of all of these challenges, marketing tends to join the party late. This is especially true at product-driven companies. Typically, the product team builds something lightweight to validate the market, has some success, and then starts iterating. At this point they realize that they need help reaching the market, and that's when the sales team is typically formed. The sales team, for its part, needs resources to support selling, which usually leads to the first marketing hire or an engagement with an outside marketing firm.

This is unfortunate because by the time the company is beginning to understand the potential of marketing, the product is already on the market—without marketing's alignment. Marketers' first experience upon joining the company is often being handed a list of demands from sales based on their immediate needs for sales tools and leads. Often, the sales organization has established a culture around its practices that is inconsistent with modern marketing and that makes it hard for marketers to broaden the conversation beyond tools and sales leads. It's the tail wagging the dog, because these needs often amount to nothing more than a collection of tactics that don't—can't—address the need to scale sales. Marketers *can* address that goal if given the chance, but it will take time.

Considering how long it takes to establish a marketing platform it's easy to understand why this is a challenging situation to walk into as a marketer.

Companies that wait to invest in marketing end up being compelled to do so by the realization that growing the sales organization further will only support linear growth. For most companies, this occurs when revenues are between $5 million and $50 million. At that point, the board must get involved to amass the organizational will to set marketing up for success. Often leaders experience sticker shock over the costs; they represent a net new expense, and catching up from behind comes at a premium. The company will probably have to maintain redundant systems during the transition. Usually, the investment in some core marketing systems and technology comes before the company has invested in hiring a senior marketing executive. Because marketing has become increasingly technology-driven, this approach can make establishing a marketing platform even more complex than it already is. Plus, there will be a period during which the sales organization needs to continue to grow while the company is pouring investment into building a marketing platform to drive scalable sales growth.

Whether you are working in a small or medium-size business or a major enterprise, the ideas presented in this book will, I hope, be valuable because they describe the direction that marketing is taking. And they are as relevant to marketers in the business-to-business (B2B) world as they are to business-to-consumer (B2C) marketers. In fact, there is a convergence taking place between these two worlds; buyers of all types now have the same expectations as the individual consumer: "We want all the information; we want to hear from the community and our peers; we want it to be more transactional, self-directed, and personalized."

3

Scaling Sales: Marketing and the Role of Automation

The aim of marketing is to make selling superfluous ... to know and understand the customer so well that the product or service fits him and sells itself.[1]

—Peter Drucker

Who would argue with this pronouncement—made more than 40 years ago—by management's legendary thinker Peter Drucker? What I really want to know is how he would respond to the question, "Is the aim of product development to make marketing superfluous?" To me, the answer has the power to transform the way we think about marketing and about business in general.

Drucker's statement implies that to scale revenue generation we must automate the work of the sales organization as much as possible by making the buyer's journey more self-service and transactional. Regardless of whether companies are pursuing this goal, customers have taken the first bit to heart, bypassing sales for most of the journey. Analyst data shows that more than half of the buyer's journey is typically completed before the buyer even reaches out to sales.[2] The challenge for marketers is to manage and influence that first leg of the buyer's journey. If marketers do not deliver experiences for the self-directed buyer, their companies will lose out to those companies that do. Many, in fact most, companies aren't doing this enough, and they're missing out.

In most companies, there are two zones of engagement for buyers in this phase of the journey: one consisting of third-party properties and the other, of owned (i.e., the company's proprietary) properties. Third-party properties, which include publications and social media channels, typically establish awareness and trigger initial demand. Companies' general objective in using them is to drive potential customers as efficiently as possible from third-party properties to owned ones where they can deliver the best experience, offer calls-to-action, and collect data to understand the prospect better.

It's typically with your owned properties—your retail locations, mobile apps, websites, and company publications—that you have the most flexibility to automate traditional sales functions and make them more self-service. Marketing automation technologies initially focused on owned properties, although that is now changing.

Marketing Automation Is a Foundational Technology

According to Steve Woods, the CTO and co-founder of Eloqua (now Oracle Marketing Cloud):

> Marketing automation is first and foremost about buyer understanding; [about getting] deep insight into buyer interests and intents, what we call the buyer's *digital body language*. The automation part involves putting together the right series of interactions—online, social, e-mail, with sales, etc.—that make sense for each type of buyer, but then automating it to deliver a unique experience for every one of millions of buyers.

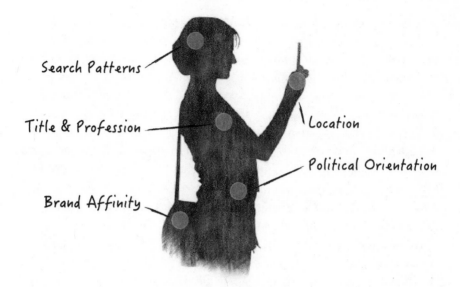

Search Patterns

Title & Profession

Brand Affinity

Location

Political Orientation

FIGURE 1.2 Digital Body Language

Take automated marketing nurture programs, for example. These are designed to educate the prospective buyer while influencing their buying decision. Nurture programs range from automated e-mails that feature everything from educational assets (such as industry guides or videos) to invitations (to online or in-person events), and mobile notifications (for discounts or other mobile-optimized content). These programs respond to how the user engages with each message or asset. For example, if in a customer's initial visit to the website, she focuses on just one product area, then you might target personalized pages that privilege content about similar products when the customer returns (assuming she allows browser cookies). If the prospect provides a phone number while registering for an event, he might get an SMS reminder before it starts. If the prospect provides an e-mail address in exchange for a guidebook then the company's follow-up messages will take the prospect's receipt of the guidebook into account. The more the prospect shares about herself during the process the more she gets back in return from the marketer.

This escalating value exchange is represented by a process called "progressive profiling," which asks for more and more information from the prospect (such as company, title, estimated time to purchase) in exchange for more and more valuable content or services (such as an invitation to an exclusive event or an opportunity to speak with a particular thought-leader). All along the way, data from the exchanges is recorded and used to identify which phase of the buyer's journey the prospect is in. A marketing automation program is a kind of tool that can help companies effectively manage more of the buyer's journey before contact with sales. Although many of the examples mentioned here refer to websites and e-mail, keep in mind that marketing automation is not e-mail-oriented but rather crosses all touchpoints and channels.

Automation platforms that support nurture programs also provide a mechanism for aligning marketing and sales. Alignment between the two functions is, of course, crucial. To understand the business value of alignment, consider what companies forgo in its absence. Various analysts report that B2B companies that are unable to align sales and marketing teams around the right processes and technologies end up forfeiting at least 10 percent of revenue every year. Combine that with the fact that, according to Demand Gen Report, "Nurtured leads produce, on average, a 20 percent increase in sales opportunities versus nonnurtured leads,"[3] and there is an even more powerful rationale for bridging the marketing/sales divide.

Getting to Alignment

It's up to marketers to design nurture programs with input from their sales colleagues. Many marketers think that marketing automation will be a slam dunk. Those who do, however, aren't fully appreciating the level of investment—in money, time, and IT skills—that is required to develop a steady flow of sales-ready leads.

Whether you build or buy, the cost of the marketing automation platform is just the tip of the iceberg. A platform is only as good as the team that's trained to use it. In addition, the platform must be integrated with your other systems. You'll likely need to expand your content team to support your nurture programs, and you'll need to do considerable experimentation in a dynamic context before the program starts generating a substantial enough lead flow, one that's comparable to that of a team of prospectors.

As the lead flow builds and qualifications grow, the marketing and sales teams will have to coordinate the transition from manual to automated. That means fighting lingering habits, such as getting salespeople to resist the temptation to call on people who are in the nurture program but who are not yet fully qualified. Marketing and sales must agree on the definitions for each stage of qualification; for example, what is the minimum qualification required for sales to engage directly?

Clearly, realizing the promise of marketing automation takes ongoing commitment and investment. To complicate matters, you can't know up front what kind of marketing automation programs will be most effective for your team and your goals. Sitting down with sales to agree on a static blueprint would be counterproductive. Instead, you need an approach that is optimized to quickly zero in on what works, based on data about how customers engage with and react to your program. You need an approach that will let you put something, however basic, out there fast, an approach that will let you quickly convert small wins into trust by putting points on the board with the sales team.

Enter Agile

Agile is optimal in situations where it's difficult, if not impossible, to accurately estimate project scope—and where a poor estimate will lead to wasted effort and squandered resources. Generally, the goal of implementing Agile in a marketing context has been, as Jim Ewel observes on his website agilemarketing.net, "to improve the speed, predictability, transparency, and adaptability of change to the marketing function."[4]

Although you can certainly harvest low-hanging fruit with your marketing automation by following best practices, such a program must be tailored to your organization to capture its full value. Furthermore, marketing automation platforms depend on inputs from your organization's other systems, such as CRM, the website, and the service back-end, in order to deliver the right experience to the right person at the right time via the right channel. But because of the fragmented technology landscape and the relative nascence of marketing technology, those systems often don't play well together. The traditional development approach is not only impractical, it's unfeasible; by the time you could get a marketing automation program implemented it would already be obsolete.

To develop a marketing automation program, the marketing organization must involve the sales organization as partner, customer, and collaborator. As such, sales can support the development of a scalable lead-engine by efficiently prototyping and validating marketing automation programs based on the team's firsthand experience. For example, the sales team can test follow-up e-mail campaigns that can be later automated to determine which subject lines and messages resonate most with specific buyer segments. Moreover, there will likely be interactions that cannot be automated (imagine trying to automate cross-enterprise sales) but that must be coordinated. This is paramount in order to avoid conflicts between automated and nonautomated interactions. Think about how awkward it would be to send a customer an automated offer by e-mail after having just closed a deal with her on the phone.

Automation Is about Amplification

With marketing automation, the goal is generally not to create new buyer behaviors so much as to take existing interactions between prospects and salespeople and make them more efficient, consistent, and targeted. To paraphrase Steve Jobs, technology is at its best when it amplifies existing human behaviors.[5] This technological amplification ideally incorporates both automation (scale) and personalization (relevance). This is the macro trend that we've seen playing out across the web as marketing technology grows more sophisticated, integrated, and complete. It's also the core promise of social networks like Facebook and search engines like Google that aim to filter out the noise from the signal and amplify only the most relevant content for each and every one of their users. With Facebook, it's based on social interactions, with Google, on a specific query (although Google has clearly expanded beyond the search function). With the ubiquitous use of services such as Facebook and Google, consumers have come to expect personalization, so companies that fail to deliver on that promise will undoubtedly be disrupted.

As businesses increasingly shift more processes online—specifically portions of the sales process into the automated marketing process—we would expect to see fewer salespeople per dollar of revenue. Indeed, the U.S. Bureau of Labor and Statistics has shown a steady decline of salespeople per dollar of GDP growth in the United States.[6] A likely corollary is that salespeople should be focusing more on higher value activities, which effectively increases their scale as a resource. This can be enormously valuable, given that there's a hard limit to the number of deals any one individual can close. Automated processes, on the other hand, have no limit. When you consider training and retention costs, adding more salespeople to increase revenue when there are existing opportunities to improve automation is shortsighted.

Part of what marketers are doing is turning lower value sales operations into services (such as prospecting-as-a-service or qualification-as-a-service). Doing so will help marketers address a lack of credibility with the business because they'll be able to more effectively attribute their impact on sales. In fact, in many cases marketing will own the entire sale, which is the single best means of establishing credibility. Today, slightly fewer than a third of top marketers surveyed by The CMO Survey reported that their companies are able to demonstrate quantitatively the impact of their marketing spending.[7] You can bet that the marketers that make up that one-third are leveraging marketing automation.

Where have we seen examples of successful automation of the sales process? The travel industry is one. And it has established clear attribution of results. The industry's salespeople (travel agents) used to sell travel, but today, most consumers buy their own travel online in a fully automated way. Yes, there are still travel agents, but they tend to focus on high-value, complex transactions. And it's not the sales organization that develops and manages such services, it's the marketing organization (along with product management).

The automation of sales functions depends on the marketer's ability to develop services that deliver relevant experiences to potential customers at scale. They must also be able to constantly update and improve these services as market conditions change and the business evolves. Unfortunately, most marketers have very limited experience with service development. Service development has traditionally been the job of the CTO, the CIO, and the chief product officer (CPO). The leaders in these roles have embraced an adaptive approach (Agile) over the last 10 to 15 years to remain competitive. So, as marketers get involved in service development, they must accept the influence of these leaders. And they must adopt adaptive approaches to deliver on the promise of the modern marketing platform and marketing-as-a-service (MaaS). In the next chapters, we'll take a deeper look at adaptive approaches and how marketers can collaborate with their peers to implement Agile in a marketing context.

4

The Rise of Agile

It is not the strongest of the species that survives, nor the most intelligent that survives. It is the one that is most adaptable to change.[1]

—Charles Darwin

In 2001, 17 developers got together to formulate the Agile Manifesto. This manifesto establishes an alternative to what they characterized as "heavyweight, documentation-driven" software development. The developers collectively represented a range of adaptive development approaches, including Extreme Programming (XP), Scrum, Dynamic Systems Development Method (DSDM), Adaptive Software Development, Crystal, Feature-Driven Development, and Pragmatic Programming. The Agile Manifesto is based on four values:

1. Individuals and interactions over processes and tools.
2. Working software over comprehensive documentation.
3. Customer collaboration over contract negotiation.
4. Responding to change over following a plan.

That is, while there is value in the items on the right, we value the items on the left more.[2]

Underlying These Values Are 12 Principles

1. Our highest priority is to satisfy the customer through early and continuous delivery of valuable software.
2. Welcome changing requirements, even late in development. Agile processes harness change for the customer's competitive advantage.
3. Deliver working software frequently, from a couple of weeks to a couple of months, with a preference for the shorter timescale.
4. Businesspeople and developers must work together daily throughout the project.
5. Build projects around motivated individuals. Give them the environment and support they need, and trust them to get the job done.
6. The most efficient and effective method of conveying information to and within a development team is face-to-face conversation.
7. Working software is the primary measure of progress.
8. Agile processes promote sustainable development. The sponsors, developers, and users should be able to maintain a constant pace indefinitely.
9. Continuous attention to technical excellence and good design enhances agility.
10. Simplicity—the art of maximizing the amount of work not done—is essential.
11. The best architectures, requirements, and designs emerge from self-organizing teams.
12. At regular intervals, the team reflects on how to become more effective, then tunes and adjusts its behavior accordingly.

On the face of it, these values and principles certainly seem software-centric enough. The values, in particular, are so general that it may not be immediately clear how they could make a difference. Which begs the question: Why is the manifesto even necessary? What were its authors rebelling against?

Before the Agile Manifesto, software development followed traditional project management approaches, all of which assume a high degree of confidence about project scope and direction. Waterfall, long the dominant approach, basically defines the end product and works backward from that point to define a detailed project plan. Such plans are linear and typically require that each phase be completed before the next one begins. Waterfall is useful when the thing that you're building is actually a building. That's because you don't typically make dramatic changes in direction once you've built 50 stories of a 100-story building!

Waterfall is one type of predictive approach. At the opposite end of the development spectrum are adaptive approaches, of which Agile is the most common. (Readers already familiar with adaptive approaches such as Agile might want to skip ahead to Chapter 8.)

In contrast to a predictive approach like Waterfall, an adaptive one does not follow a straight path from point A to point B. Rather, it takes one step toward point B and then pivots as necessary to reorient to the position of B based on updated input. Adaptive methods acknowledge that point B may be moving or may not be where it was originally thought to be (see Figure 1.3).

Agile is optimal for complex situations in which uncertainty is high: uncertainty about the scope and even about whether the product or service meets a market need. Today, a handful of adaptive methods are being used by companies in a broad range of circumstances. I'll discuss some of the most popular ones including XP, Scrum, and Kanban in Part II. In the meantime, let's explore how predictive and adaptive approaches compare with each other, starting with Figure 1.4.

Agile is an adaptive approach quite simply because it is designed to maximize your ability to absorb changes in scope and direction. But Agile and Waterfall are not mutually exclusive.

One of my first jobs out of college was working for Blaine Bershad, the lead architect at a Boston-based firm. Blaine had been a contractor for

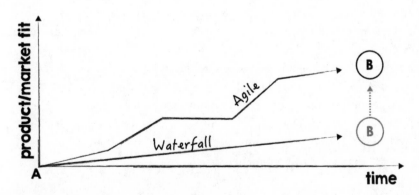

FIGURE 1.3 Agile vs Waterfall Process

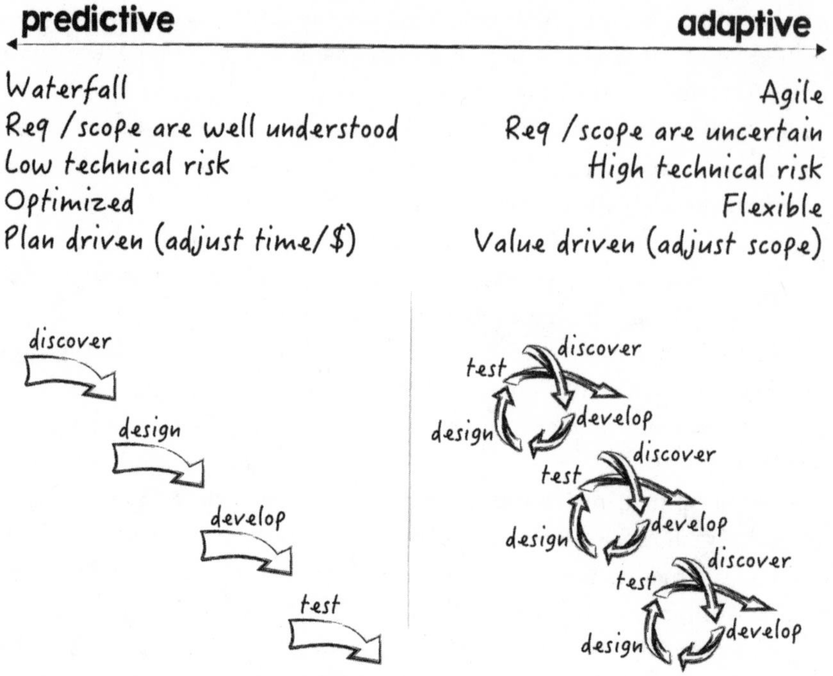
predictive
adaptive
Waterfall
Req / scope are well understood
Low technical risk
Optimized
Plan driven (adjust time/$)
Agile
Req / scope are uncertain
High technical risk
Flexible
Value driven (adjust scope)
discover
design
develop
test
discover
test
develop
design
discover
test
develop
design
discover
test
develop
design

FIGURE 1.4 Waterfall Compared to Agile

many years before becoming a licensed architect, and had spent many years building ski-in/ski-out condominiums in the hills around New England ski resorts. After constructing dozens of condos, the basic architectural footprint remained the same, but Blaine continued to refine many aspects of the design to make it better and better. The inhabitants of his last set of condos benefited from the many insights Blaine acquired and the many optimizations and innovations he developed over the years. Here, Blaine embedded a Waterfall process inside a larger Agile process. It's possible to do the reverse, as well—something many marketers applying Agile will have to embrace, because Agile is not necessarily a good fit for every marketing activity.

So, predictive and adaptive methodologies fall on a continuum. They are not black and white. They can be combined and embedded into each other.

When we speak of development, there are approaches, methods, and practices. Let's clarify the nomenclature:

- An *approach* represents a philosophy or conceptual orientation as to how development is done. Agile is an approach.

- A *method* is a practice or set of practices that are consistent with an approach. For example, we discuss a range of Agile methodologies, including Scrum and Kanban.
- *Practices* are specific activities comprising a method. An individual or group engages in practices that collectively represent a method.
- *Transformation* refers to the process of implementing an approach—for our purposes, an adaptive approach—at the organizational or enterprise level.

Why the Shift to Agile?

Adaptive approaches have been gaining market share for some time (and not just in the software space). Why? Here are four big reasons:

1. **The need for speed over size.** Today, technology evolves at an ever-increasing rate. Faster innovation cycles have led to the evolution of business and distribution models. Remember how quickly the music industry moved from CDs to online sales to music-as-a-service (e.g., Pandora and Spotify)? Agile is built for speed.

2. **The rise of open-source and distributed development.** Increasingly, the market prefers technologies that are ubiquitous and commonly understood. This guarantees that talent will be available in the marketplace, which facilitates growth, resilience, and adaptivity. Consider for example, that there are over 9 million Java developers in the world, which makes it one of the most popular open-source server side programming language. But it's not just about specific technologies or languages; people open-source design as well. And it's also about the collaborative Agile practices that surround open source and make it possible. Agile has reached critical mass with practitioners in the open-source movement and is itself becoming a common practice.

3. **The availability of low-cost development resources.** Agile favors standard, granular, and interchangeable parts over custom parts. Where adaptivity is critical, Agile supports the ability to obtain and replace parts quickly and reliably, thus preventing potential bottlenecks associated with changes to tooling or equipment. The increasing availability of low-cost commodity resources (such as computing hardware) has lowered the barrier to entry, enabling upstarts to compete with established firms. Agile

has gained momentum, for example, with the maker movement (low-cost 3D printing) as the cost of prototyping has come down.

4. **The distribution of computing power at the edge of the network (the Internet of Things).** Agile has a thirst for immediate feedback and offers the ability to iterate products and services even if they are dispersed throughout the market. This is an alternative to an environment where the technology at the edge of the network is hard-coded and not updatable. We now have the ability to embed supercomputers into so many things, from cars to watches to smoke detectors. At the same time, there's a lot of uncertainty about whether such products will even work (or whether people will use such services in unintended ways) when they are deployed at scale. Agile gives innovators critical feedback while also mitigating some risks.

CASE STUDY: ALL IN ONE—ADAPTIVE RISK MANAGEMENT AND ENABLING INNOVATION

The Nest Protect home fire detector offers a good example of Agile's value at the edge of the network. Initially, the product was designed so that users could silence an alarm by waving their hands below the detector. But it was discovered that in some cases smoke could fool the detector into silencing itself. Nest was able to act quickly to remotely disable this feature. In this case, iteration at the edge of the network protected the Nest Protect from a catastrophic safety defect.

That said, it's still very early-stage, and companies can't always sufficiently address defects with a software update. True, Nest was able to avoid catastrophe in this case, but the company also experienced some issues that could not be resolved with a software update. Thousands of Nest Protect units have experienced false positive alarms within six months of being activated. To make matters worse, the user has to remove the unit from the ceiling to disable the alarm in these situations. Here, the issue was a faulty sensor, which required a hardware replacement.

Had Nest been unable to address the first issue with a software update, the company might not be around today. The second issue,

(continued)

(*continued*)

however, will require extraordinary customer service and support to resolve. Granted, early adopters are more tolerant of such issues than the rest of the market, but this example shows that companies are just beginning to learn how much risk management and innovation is possible when they are product-adapting at the edge of the network.

This practice is a high-stakes game for companies like Tesla, which is embedding hardware in its cars to support sophistacted self-driving features that are intended to be incrementally enabled over time. Thus far, the company has been able to deploy an auto-park feature for parallel parking and an "autopilot" feature that allows the car to semi-autonomously drive. The Tesla release notes state that drivers must maintain contact with the steering wheel, but there is ample evidence on social media that some drivers are ignoring this advice. It remains to be seen if Telsa will release an update that will fundamentally overhaul the product experience with fully autonomous driving. Must currently forcasest that this will be available within three years.

These four reasons for Agile's growing acceptance reflect a larger trend: the trade-off of optimization in favor of flexibility. This trade-off is apparent within specific Agile methods that are very engineering-oriented, such as XP, which promotes the development of granular bits of general functionality over more complex, specific, and highly optimized bits. XP also specifies many coding practices that make it possible for any developer to understand any other developer's code and to increase knowledge-sharing. In other words, Agile has baked-in practices that reflect these trends.

Agile as Competitive Advantage

Companies that embrace Agile do so because of the competitive advantage it offers to those competing in rapidly evolving markets. And consumers have quickly adjusted their expectations based on companies that do this well. Consumers are also much more likely to be vocal on social networks about companies that fail to meet their expectations. They have become accustomed to consumer application experiences (such as Facebook's mobile application) that change on an almost daily basis. They've also gotten used to reporting bugs and then seeing them disappear. Offloading some of the quality assurance to the user community has allowed Agile teams to work faster while building stronger relationships with end users. This is part of shortening the feedback loop between the market and the company. From a marketer's perspective, feedback loops that are used to validate an incremental product release are compatible with the larger process of validating product/market fit. They also set up a massive opportunity to leverage the community as a platform for promoting adoption of the product or service—assuming, of course, that you're delivering a good one. If you can effectively respond to feedback, customers are inherently more likely to advocate for your product or service. Stated simply, your products or services will reflect customers' input, thus giving them a sense of ownership and investment.

End-user engagement is not only desirable, it is necessary for hastening innovation. Closer contact with consumers leads to more direct feedback and insights about potential service features and direction. It's a virtuous feedback loop. This is basically what underpins the second, third, and fourth principles in the manifesto: ("working software over comprehensive documentation, customer collaboration over contract negotiation, responding to change over following a plan"). Interestingly, the first principle ("individuals and interactions over processes and tools") is an example of an internal feedback loop that is actually being shortened.

In fact, to conform to Agile principles, feedback loops must be implemented on multiple levels. Developers, too, must foster closer collaboration amongst themselves that ideally includes colocation and pair programming (although more tools are emerging that facilitate such practices for remote workers). Pair programming is an XP practice in which two developers literally write code together: the "driver" writes code while the "observer" reviews each line of code as it is typed in and references the requirements. The two programmers switch roles frequently. As a low-level feedback loop, pair programming has several documented advantages, including improved quality and increased knowledge sharing.

Pair programming represents the lowest level of promoting feedback at the code level (one developer providing feedback to the other). Internal testers or beta testers might provide feedback at the feature level (designers and testers provide feedback to developers). Customers provide feedback on incremental releases at product or service level (external customer data and/or customer support provides feedback to development).

Establishing feedback loops at multiple levels is one example of an Agile practice that can be applied with relative ease in the marketing context. Many other practices do not translate as readily. When I say that Agile practices are impacting marketing practices I am not suggesting that marketers literally adopt developers' practices letter for letter—that one marketer, for instance, works on some messaging copy with another at his side reviewing the content in real time (although that might be an interesting experiment). I am saying that closer internal collaboration and a closer connection to customers is essential, and it's useful for marketers to take a page from development's book on this topic.

If you identify what underpins any specific practice (e.g., the foundational values and principles of Agile), you can get ideas about how to translate it to a marketing context. More broadly, I'm suggesting that marketers think of their work environment more as that of a start-up than a mature business. They have to, considering the tremendous amount of innovation that's taking place in the marketing technology industry.

Is Agile Marketing the Future? A Pulse Check

All kinds of conferences, blogs, and podcasts with titles containing the terms "agile marketing" (or "marketing agility") have been popping up lately. Whether or not the term agile marketing gains currency, the Agile approach *is* already having a pronounced impact on marketing practices and platforms.

To put this in perspective, consider the Google Trends data in Figure 1.5. Today agile marketing is still a relatively low-volume search term compared to inbound marketing. Inbound marketing, or what Seth Godin calls "permission marketing," consists of marketing programs that work by pull rather than push: Potential

(continued)

(*continued*)

customers initiate the buyers' journey by requesting information. Essentially, these are opt-in programs that focus on educating buyers while also nurturing and qualifying them. Interestingly, while the Agile approach supports inbound marketing (and marketing automation in general), it has not developed the same kind of awareness in the marketplace (see Figure 1.5).[3]

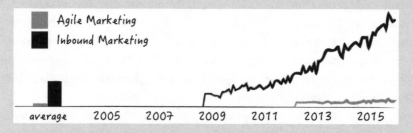

FIGURE 1.5 Google Trends: 'Agile Marketing' vs 'Inbound Marketing'

Now that you understand how Agile methods work—and how and why Agile is transforming marketing—what do you need to do to get started with Agile? I never promised this book would be a detailed guide, but I can offer a simple road map. Follow these six steps:

1. **Ask around, talk it up.** Inform your peers that you're implementing Agile and find out if any of them have experience with Agile. If so, talk to them about how they used it. Enlist their help as you develop your program. (If none of your peers have used it, you can do them a service: Set their expectations about Agile by giving them this book!)
2. **Appoint or hire an Agile leader.** If there's someone available in your organization who has extensive experience with Agile, appoint that person to help you implement it. If not, consider hiring an Agile coach to help you lead your initial implementation.
3. **Create a game plan, assemble your resources.** Pick a good starter project, select an Agile method, and assemble an Agile team. Then be sure to post the Agile Marketing Manifesto in a visible place.
4. **Complete an iteration.** Do one round of design, build, test, and feedback-gathering.
5. **Share your results.** Communicate the results and feedback in the most transparent way possible (say, with a visible Kanban board and a metrics dashboard).
6. **Return to step 4 and repeat.**

Adaptive Methods for Modernizing Marketing

5

A Snapshot of Leading Methods

Not all Agile methods are appropriate for all contexts. And the method that ends up working best for your team will likely be different from the one you started with. That's because methods must be adapted to your team, your culture, your projects, and your goals. This evolution is baked into Agile through a retrospective process that periodically evaluates how Agile is working and how it can be improved.

There is something meta about this aspect of Agile because part of what allows Agile to accommodate change (to function in rapidly evolving contexts) is the fact that its ability to change is part of its DNA. Agile is a dynamic (if structured) approach. Agile does not change for change's sake; it changes in response to feedback that shows that change is needed. And when Agile is working well, it settles into a consistent rhythm.

As with any approach, Agile has its advantages and disadvantages. It is not suited to every project or context. It works very well for services that are always on (like marketing automation), moderately well for programs that have a regular cadence (like a monthly webinar), and least well for one-off initiatives.

The established Agile methods that are popular today differ considerably in their degree of structure as well as in the specific contexts in which they are applied. More structured methods like XP are, for instance, very engineering-oriented and prescribe detailed practices for writing code. Scrum is somewhat less prescriptive than XP, and can be applied outside

FIGURE 2.1 Range of Agile Methods

of software development, while Kanban is the least prescriptive and most broadly applicable (see Figure 2.1).

The next two chapters provide a foundation on Agile methods. In Chapter 6 we'll examine the Scrum method, which was the first to gain significant traction with marketers. That's partly because it is a project management-oriented method and also because it is popular with development teams. You'll not only learn how prescriptive the method is, you'll learn about how time is its key constraint.

In Chapter 7 we'll explore a less prescriptive method known as Kanban. This method emerged from manufacturing, not from the software industry. Kanban incorporates many Scrum practices, but operates under a different key constraint: work-in-progress (WIP). We'll also look at XP, which is at the highly prescriptive end of the spectrum.

Throughout these two chapters are representative examples of how each method works and how the methods differ. I also compare and contrast these methods so that you'll have a sense of how they relate to each other and how the elements of each can be used to develop your own method. Keep in mind, however, that these chapters are not intended to be a comprehensive guide to launching an implementation; they are meant to give you a grounding in the adaptive methods referenced throughout the book.

6   The Skinny on Scrum

I often tell people who are interested in Agile that a good way to learn Agile methods is to start thinking like a product or service developer. Select a service you'd like to design and build: a nurture program, a portfolio of sales collateral, an advertisement, a website, or even an event series. Then list everything you'd need to do to get the most basic version of this service created. This can seem overwhelming at first, but it doesn't have to be if you apply the most fundamental Agile practice: list your user stories.

It might surprise you to hear that you're probably already using this most fundamental Agile practice. It's something that almost everyone does when they feel like they have too much to do. They start by making a list of everything they need to do; then they size up all of the tasks and order them by priority. Just doing this tends to make people feel better because they've gone from the anxiety associated with facing an undefined effort to the comfort associated with knowing a well-defined set of tasks.

Agile developers call these tasks *user stories* or just stories. In a development and marketing context, user stories explain the end result of the task from the end user's (that is, the customer's) perspective. That, of course, helps keep the user's needs central to the design. An example of a high-level task is "users who return to our website should be presented with information based on their previous visit." High-level tasks get broken down into more detailed ones as you assess and prioritize them. The items at the top of your list should be the most detailed.

Scrum: A Service Development Method

Scrum is the most popular Agile method used by development teams today. One of Scrum's key principles is that it privileges regularity of releases over scope. In other words, it's better to release on time than to delay a release in order to complete more work. When you translate this notion to the context of your list, sprint planning involves drawing a line under the last task that you can realistically perform within a specific time frame. To accomplish this, you'll have to have estimated the time needed to complete each story so that you can add up what is realistically possible within each iteration or timebox. That's what you'll execute on during your first Agile iteration, or what Scrum calls a *sprint*. If you overestimated what can be done in your sprint you'll have to remove an item from your list or trim down some items so that you can release on time. In Agile parlance, this is called reducing the *scope* of the sprint. Sprints can vary in length but usually run between one and four weeks. What matters is that they are regular and set a steady cadence for your work and releases. Between iterations, you'll evaluate which stories you'll implement in the next iteration.

In fact, between iterations you'll have a chance to review, estimate, prioritize, and order everything under the line that defined your first iteration. All those stories are called your *backlog*; the process of organizing, estimating, prioritizing, and breaking high-level stories into detailed ones is called *grooming*. During this process you'll adjust your direction based on what you've learned in the retrospective of the first iteration. This retrospective includes a review of the data you've collected from what you've built so far or direct user feedback.

Scrum also dictates that the elements within your iteration should amount to something useable or at least testable. This is important because Scrum requires feedback to validate each release, but without a useable release, it's difficult to obtain the feedback required to validate direction.

Most Scrum teams use some kind of tool to manage their stories; there are many solutions on the market that work. For software development, my favorites are Jira and Pivotal Tracker; for marketing, I prefer Asana because it's more general-purpose. Such tools function as the substrate for your Agile practice. They include representations of your initiatives, stories, timeboxes, and backlogs.

Key Scrum Practices

Following are reference definitions for some of the practices associated with the Scrum method that we cover in this chapter:

- **Sprint:** The sprint is an Agile iteration and contains a collection of stories that have been estimated and prioritized to fit within a designated time period or timebox. The length of the sprint is consistent from one to the next and typically ranges between one and four weeks.
- **Scrum:** This is not only the name of an Agile methodology, but it's also the name given to the brief stand-up meeting that the meeting leader (Scrum Master) runs every day. At this meeting, participants report on three items: (1) what they accomplished since the last check-in; (2) what they will accomplish before the next check-in; and (3) what roadblocks might impede their progress. For the marketing context, I've added two more: (4) what they think is currently working well, and (5) what's not.
- **User story:** A story is a short articulation in plain language that captures what a user does—or needs to do—that your product is attempting to solve. It allows the product owner (generally, the business owner) to capture in a concise fashion the who, what, and why of a requirement. User stories also ensure that the item being built is centered on the users and their needs.
- **Functional specification:** A functional specification is a detailed document that outlines engineering requirements. In a marketing context, however, it is more like a business requirements document (BRD) that might support an initiative.
- **Backlog:** The backlog is a list of stories that have not yet been assigned to a sprint. Items in the backlog should be estimated and prioritized by the product owner. In the marketing context, the business owner would do this

(continued)

(continued)

prioritization, as he or she is the one assessing the return against the required investment

- **Timeboxing:** Timeboxing allocates a fixed time period to each sprint and privileges releasing on time over releasing a set scope of work. On the plus side, this supports a regular release schedule. But it makes it difficult to predict exactly when specific feature releases will occur. In the marketing context, timeboxing can be a challenge when managing against real-world events such as holidays. Once comfortable with adjusting scope, however, it's almost always possible to release something on time.

- **Retrospective:** A retrospective is a debriefing held by a project team at the end of a project or iteration. In it, the team discusses what was successful about the effort, what could be improved, and how to incorporate findings in future iterations or projects. The retrospective focuses on the product being developed as well as on the process of development itself.

- **Planning poker:** Planning poker (or Scrum Poker) is a consensus-based technique for estimating stories. In planning poker, members of the group make estimates by placing numbered cards face down on the table. Instead of calling them out loud, the cards are flipped over once they are all on the table and the estimates are then discussed. By hiding the estimates until they are all submitted, the group can avoid *anchoring*, the cognitive bias in which the first number spoken aloud sets a precedent for subsequent estimates. Typically the cards represent a Fibonacci sequence including a zero: 0, 1, 2, 3, 5, 8, 13, 21, 34, 55, 89 to reflect the inherent uncertainty in estimating larger items (see in Chapter 8).

- **Velocity tracking:** Velocity tracking is a measure of how quickly a team or individual is working though stories—so stories must be estimated and tracked upon completion. To establish benchmarks for measuring, velocity tracking typically requires each story to have multiple iterations.

(continued)

(continued)

- **Burndown chart:** A burndown chart is a graphical representation of work remaining versus time remaining. The outstanding work is often depicted on the y (vertical) axis, with time remaining plotted along the x (horizontal) axis. Some task management solutions like Asana, Jira, and Pivotal Tracker offer burndown charts as a feature. The burndown chart is very useful for project management and can serve as an Agile alternative to Gantt Charts, which are used for Waterfall methodologies.

If you're interested in learning more, you'll find a complete directory of Agile practices for development at http://guide .agilealliance.org/.

How Scrum Works in a Marketing Context

In software development, the Waterfall approach has four broad phases: discovery/analysis, design, development, and testing. Waterfall progresses through these stages once and then delivers the final product. Agile has the same phases, but instead of progressing through them in serial fashion, it repeats them continuously, releasing an incrementally more complete product with each iteration.

To understand Scrum's application in a marketing context, consider that our product or initiative is a new section of a website or a new landing page template. With Waterfall, this would go pretty much the same way as the traditional approach to product development that I described in the book's introduction. You start with your business requirements document, which you give to design. Design passes the page over to development, which then tests it for release. All throughout, the product owner, or business lead, might not have checked in on the process until nearly the end of the project.

The Agile process (in this case Scrum) would be different from the start, because you'd be focused on just what you can build within a single sprint for a first release. And, you might not expose all end users to the release. Rather you'd direct a small amount of traffic to the page to support iteration and then release it more broadly as you roll out more functionality. During your first sprint, discovery/analysis, design, develop, and testing are happening concurrently. As the page owner, you'd be involved during the entire process so that you could catch any missed requirements, discover unexpected interactions, and ensure that the experience on the website is right.

By following this method, you would have your initial release much sooner. True, it will be basic, but you'll also start generating feedback sooner. Indeed, in many cases you'll have your second iteration done before the Waterfall approach would have produced a single release. And that means you're either getting to value or failing and adjusting faster. Much of the time, there will be something right out of the gate that needs adjustment.

The Cost of Bad Predictions

When teams rely on Waterfall for web projects, they typically rely on supposed best practices and individual opinion over direct user feedback. Even though they conduct reviews during the development process, that's not enough to overcome the bias inherent in best practices and opinion, both of which are secondhand sources. And this bias is precisely what prevents these teams from discovering market realities that are inconsistent with their projections of reality. The Agile approach, on the other hand, has built-in processes for scrutinizing key performance data, which keeps teams grounded in reality.

The value of taking an iterative approach is that your original plan will not perfectly reflect what gets built because of the adjustments made as a result of feedback. And this introduces three simple truths about development:

1. It is impossible to gather all the requirements at the beginning of a project.
2. Whatever requirements you do gather are guaranteed to change.
3. There will always be more to do than time and money will allow.[1]

(continued)

(*continued*)

That last truth points to the value associated with privileging the timebox over scope. With the Waterfall approach, the later in the process you make changes the more expensive they will be. However, with Agile you tend to discover changes earlier, which reduces cost. Moreover, the approach itself is fundamentally optimized to absorb change—a feature that reduces the cost of change throughout the project (see Figure 2.2).

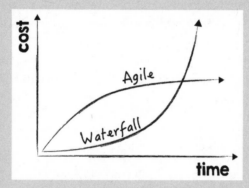

FIGURE 2.2 Cost of Change

Scrum Is a Team Sport

With Scrum projects, your designers will participate in creating user stories, developers will end up working on the design, and testers will work with development to build tests into the code. That's not to say that each team member does not have specific areas of expertise and sign-off authority (you can have that if you really want). But it does acknowledge that the person who designed a solution will bring a unique perspective to how it is tested. Of course, the person who developed the solution will also have value to add during testing. In fact, testing is a phase in which everyone on the team participates.

Scrum splits your organization into small, cross-functional teams that self-organize around process. And it splits the work into a list of small, discrete deliverables. Further, it splits development into short, fixed-length sprints. Most Agile methods call for cross-functional teams, but Scrum defines two management roles: the Product Owner and Scrum Master. The former is essentially the business owner and the person responsible for prioritizing what gets built and the final requirements. It's a challenging role because this person must reconcile many inputs and make numerous trade-offs. (Interestingly, in the development context, marketers are often the ones providing input to Product Owners.) The Scrum Master is like a project manager whose job it is to make sure that the team is leveraging Agile practices effectively and working toward sprint goals. The Scrum Master runs a daily Scrum or stand-up meeting to keep the team aligned. In many respects, the Scrum Master is a facilitator who is both a resource for the team and a monitor who is keeping it on track.

Because Scrum is a project management-oriented framework, there is general alignment between the roles associated with a development project and a marketing project.

Development	Marketing
Product Owner	Business Owner
Scrum Master	Project Manager
Designer	Designer/Product Marketer
Development	Development/Operations
Testing	Testing

If you think about, it the roles associated with building and iterating on a website are not really that different from the roles associated with developing a service. That's because the website is, in fact, a service. With Scrum, you organize cross-functional teams around initiatives rather than organizing teams by area of expertise (such as all the designers in a design group). This is one of the most challenging aspects of implementing Scrum. The good news is that you don't have to make the switch overnight; you can instead start with a single team and transition more and more people into cross-functional teams as you go.

What we've described here should give you enough details about the Scrum method to make it more tangible—and to start a conversation with your development peers.

7 Kanban: Lean Meets Agile

Some marketing programs just won't fit nicely into the structure of Scrum, and that's okay. The goal here should not be to force everything into one method. Agile offers a range of methods that you can tailor to your organization or individual initiatives. Scrum will be better suited to certain projects, and Kanban to others. For some projects, a combination of the two would be best. For a few, predictive methods like Waterfall would be a better fit. That's why it's important to familiarize yourself with a range of methods so you can apply the right one to the job.

Two examples illustrate this point. The first comes directly from my experience working in the social technology industry and with big brands to manage their social presence and listening programs. This is an environment in which being agile (lowercase *a*, as in rapid response) is critical and well-suited for an Agile method (capital *A*, as in the approach). While it may be possible to plan strategic initiatives that will run for several months, things change quickly based on social engagement. Consider Wieden+Kennedy's ad campaign for Old Spice, widely known as "The Man Your Man Could Smell Like." It started as a traditional campaign, with a handful of commercials featuring actor and former athlete Isaiah Mustafa as the Old Spice Man. These spots triggered a flood of YouTube comments, tweets, and questions on Yahoo! Answers, which, in turn, prompted the ad agency to produce what ended up to be more than 180 videos featuring Mustafa. Neither Wieden+Kennedy nor Old Spice could have foreseen this level of success (or the sheer number of consumer and media responses) that resulted from those original commercials. Yet, week after week, they were able to crank out brilliant response videos and tweets, none of them part of the original plan, that kept the campaign front and center on the Internet. While the original spots may have been developed with a Waterfall approach, the responses clearly could not have been.

Compare the Old Spice ad to an example from my tenure at Adina, the beverage company, where trade shows were a critical component of the marketing mix. Companies like Adina had to reserve space on the trade show floor a full year in advance in order to get a decent location. With significant down payments and huge cancellation fees, we had no choice but to plan that far in advance. But while the backbone of the process was Waterfall, we approached our booth experience for the event in an Agile fashion. During the year we iterated on the layout and we even built modular components that we tested at smaller events. But we had to lock in our booth design months in advance to plan effectively for the logistics associated with manufacturing, shipping, installation, storage, and so forth.

Distinct Origins, Shared Philosophy

Technically, Kanban isn't part of the Agile tradition, although it is consistent with Agile values and principles. Kanban comes from Lean, a manufacturing approach focused on eliminating waste in the production process. In the previous chapter I showed how Agile limits the costs associated with making incremental changes in direction arising from feedback (and minimizing cost is, in effect, a form of minimizing waste). Lean is even more focused on waste reduction.

Lean emerged from the Japanese manufacturing industry. In its earliest incarnation, as part of the Toyota Production System (TPS), it identified seven specific causes of waste in the manufacturing process. These causes have been expanded on over time, as the Lean approach caught on throughout other industries. Now, many of those causes are directly relevant to marketers.

Despite its manufacturing roots, Kanban is frequently applied in the same contexts as Scrum. In some ways, it is even more appropriate for marketers than Scrum, as we will see. Kanban tracks work-in-progress (WIP) and visually represents the progression of work (i.e., stories) throughout each phase

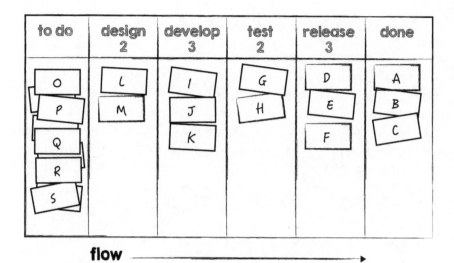

FIGURE 2.3 Kanban Board

of production as cards on a board. In Lean parlance, these cards are called Kanban cards. Moreover, unlike Scrum, Kanban does not prescribe time-boxing. Rather, Kanban is constrained by the number of items that can be handled in each development stage at any one time.

This limits the number of stories or Kanban cards that can be posted in any one column on the board at any one time (each column represents a stage of development). A work item cannot progress to the next column until there is an open slot available in that column (see Figure 2.3). Where Scrum measures velocity (the total number of story points per iteration), Kanban measures the average time it takes for an item to progress across the board, otherwise known as its cycle time.

In the context of software development and marketing, Kanban is effective for monitoring and maintaining progress because it adds transparency to the status of any story or initiative. It also helps identify bottlenecks and other inefficiencies in the process by giving them a visible form: The Agile tools mentioned earlier visually represent each initiative as it progresses through the process for both Kanban and Scrum. As we know, humans are much better at identifying patterns visually than in any other way. This makes sense: Our neurological systems for processing information visually significantly predate our ability to articulate through language. In short, we are wired for visualization, which is one reason why the Kanban board is so powerful.

Both Lean and the Kanban methodology rely on feedback loops to improve the product or service as well as the process by which it is being developed. In fact, Lean prescribes dedicating a Kaizen, or continuous improvement, team to focus on the production process. Kaizen is a daily process focused on making small improvements that collectively make a big impact. Kaizen is what allows Toyota line-workers to stop the entire production line if they find anything that is causing defects, hazards, or other forms of waste. The Kaizen team immediately investigates and resolves such issues when production stops. Having a dedicated Kaizen team is unique to Lean, but addressing process feedback periodically should sound familiar: It's a process-level internal Agile feedback loop.

Scrum versus Kanban: Similarities and Differences

How does Kanban compare with Scrum? To give you a concrete idea, the Old Spice response videos that Wieden+Kennedy created would likely have been better done with Kanban than with Scrum because the quality of the finished spots was more important than a consistent release schedule. But for Adina's trade shows, we were able to use Scrum (to test the marketing components at smaller recurring events held at our retailers' locations) within a Waterfall approach (to solidify the final event design). That's because we had firm release dates all along the way. And this speaks to the complex circumstances in which marketers work. Further, even within Agile, different methods will work in different circumstances.

Kanban does not, however, prescribe the Product Owner or Scrum Master roles nor does it require that team roles blur to the degree that Scrum prescribes. That said, Kanban implementations often incorporate many elements from Scrum such as iterations, cross-functional teams, and a daily stand-up meeting. Conversely, Scrum teams often use virtual Kanban boards to add transparency to the development process.

One advantage Kanban offers over Scrum involves estimation. Even with estimation practices like Planning Poker, people are generally bad at estimating work. As a result, they often overcommit, which can create considerable pressure at the end of each sprint. That pressure leads to burnout and finger-pointing during retrospectives. Kanban doesn't tend to have this cyclical increase and decrease in pressure (unless you are using timeboxes). The productive pressure in Kanban actually stems from maintaining cycle time; although Scrum tracks velocity, the main productive pressure with this method stems from what's been committed to in the sprint.

But this very advantage of Kanban—eliminating the cyclical time pressures—is also a disadvantage: The sense of urgency that drives production is more abstract. This is but one of the many small differences among Agile methods and reinforces the importance of choosing, combining, and implementing methods that work well in your context.

One common denominator between Scrum and Kanban is that they are both pull-oriented. Both methods pull work from a backlog when the current work items are complete. And this reflects a convergence that is taking place between Agile and Lean. Mary and Tom Poppendiek's book, *Lean Software Development: An Agile Toolkit*, has prompted active discussion about how these two approaches relate to each other. In my view, they share an underlying philosophy but consist of unique methods and practices. Overall, though, they are more similar than different. So from here on in, when I use the term Agile, know that it represents both Agile and Lean.

Once you're ready to start preparing to implement an Agile practice I strongly recommend reading Henrik Kniberg and Mattias Skarin's publication entitled *Kanban and Scrum, Making the Most of Both*.[1] This book, available for free online, is a practical desk reference for anyone implementing an Agile practice. Here is an excerpt in which the authors provide a summary comparison of Scrum and Kanban:

Similarities

- Both are Lean and Agile.
- Both use pull scheduling.
- Both limit WIP.
- Both use transparency to drive process improvement.
- Both focus on delivering releasable software [product/service] early and often.
- Both are based on self-organizing teams.
- Both require breaking the work into pieces.
- In both cases the release plan is continuously optimized based on empirical data (velocity/lead time).

Differences

Scrum	Kanban
Timeboxed iterations prescribed.	Timeboxed iterations optional. Can have separate cadences for planning, release, and process improvement. Can be event-driven instead of timeboxed.
Team commits to a specific amount of work for this iteration.	Commitment optional.
Uses velocity as default metric for planning and process improvement.	Uses lead time as default metric for planning and process improvement.
Cross-functional teams prescribed.	Cross-functional teams optional. Specialist teams allowed.
Items must be broken down so they can be completed within one sprint.	No particular item size is prescribed.
Burndown chart prescribed.	No particular type of diagram is prescribed.
WIP limited indirectly (per sprint).	WIP limited directly (per workflow state).
Estimation prescribed.	Estimation optional.
Cannot add items to ongoing iteration.	Can add new items whenever capacity is available.
A sprint backlog is owned by one specific team.	A Kanban board may be shared by multiple teams or individuals.
Prescribes three roles (Product Owner, Scrum Master, team).	Doesn't prescribe any roles.
A Scrum board is reset between each sprint.	A Kanban board is persistent.
Prescribes a prioritized product backlog.	Prioritization is optional.

CASE STUDY: READYTALK TAKES ON MARKETING AUTOMATION WITH SCRUMBAN

Few marketers have more experience applying Agile in a marketing context than Mike McKinnon, formerly the director of marketing operations for ReadyTalk, an audio and web-conferencing company. His team had been applying Agile to marketing automation and other programs for over five years. Their journey is representative of that of many other companies I've talked to throughout my research for this book.

Mike's team ran a wide variety of marketing automation programs including persona and use-case-based nurture tracks, trial and demo-based nurture tracks, and reengagement tracks, as well as webinar support campaigns for customers using its Cloud Connectors in the Oracle Marketing Cloud (OMC).

Mike described the development process for the persona-based nurture program, which was his most ambitious one. "The track was 22 programs in the program builder with over 60 shared filters and 30 shared lists. To build something of this complexity, Agile provided leverage throughout the process." As you'd expect, iterations were based on A/B tests of e-mail, content, and landing page performance. Waterfall could never have worked for this program, Mike contended. "I could not imagine building something of this scale and complexity without an Agile approach."

ReadyTalk started implementing Agile to address common challenges, such as poor coordination (owing to organizational silos), a lack of strategic focus (due to insufficient transparency), and a reactive posture (the result of constantly shifting priorities). Like most marketers who adopt Agile, they discover that it cannot only be interpreted for the marketing context; it must also be tailored to the organization.

As ReadyTalk has grown from 20 employees to more than 200, the company has used Agile not only to manage its marketing programs, but also to iterate on the process itself. This continuous

(continued)

(*continued*)

improvement has brought ReadyTalk through more than 10 iterations of Agile methods including both Scrum and Kanban.

Like many pioneers of Agile marketing, ReadyTalk started with Scrum. Five years ago, few marketers were using Kanban, and most of the guidance from development organizations was based on Scrum. ReadyTalk discovered, however, that Scrum was too process-intensive and complex; two-week sprints were not always a good fit for its programs. So Mike led his team toward the less prescriptive end of the spectrum and tried Kanban before eventually iterating to a hybrid method known as *Scrumban*. This hybrid incorporates elements of Kanban, such as limits to the number of items being worked on (work-in-process), alongside elements of Scrum, such as cross-functional teams. Interestingly, after gaining experience with Kanban, Mike's team was more able to embrace some of the more prescriptive elements of Scrum.

A big part of Mike's success with Agile had to do with keeping the marketing Scrum aligned with the product group's Scrum. They achieved this through the physical proximity of their Scrum meetings and their Kanban boards. They also embedded Scrum participants throughout the organization.

Further, to support ongoing alignment with strategic goals, all items on marketing's Kanban board were linked to a primary strategic goal. This is essential, because ReadyTalk maintains an annual planning cycle for which it sets revenue goals, as well as quarterly planning sessions in which it commits to projects and campaigns.

As a private company, ReadyTalk has also demonstrated that Agile is not anathema to annual budgeting. While it does set constraints on how aggressively the company can invest in new initiatives, it is possible to manage against a set budget. Still, the marketing plans are iterated on a quarterly basis, which is more consistent with the Agile approach.

Integrating Agile methods into the marketing practice has helped ReadyTalk break down silos within the product team, while also establishing shared priorities. According to Mike, this increased

(*continued*)

> *(continued)*
>
> organizational transparency and also provided a "tangible view into how each person is making an impact on the overall company" and "gives people the satisfaction of visibly moving tasks from the 'doing' to the 'done' column." This also facilitates the on-boarding of new team members, which has been essential for the company's rapid growth. Perhaps the greatest testament to the marketing team's success is that they've inspired other internal organizations to adopt Agile in support of their functions.

Let me offer one last thought on the Agile practices that I've just outlined. Even with less prescriptive methods, Agile may feel like a lot of process. And marketers often equate bureaucratic process as being anathema to creativity.

The concern is understandable but irrelevant. For one thing, Agile teams don't diminish the role of design. Rather, design gets to engage more deeply on an ongoing basis precisely because of the iterative process. Design, of course, is a highly creative process, so having design continue throughout the iteration means more room for creativity as well. Furthermore, for those who implement Scrum, blending team roles tends to bring cross-disciplinary attention to design and to the creative process—which adds value.

This value is two-way: while alternative perspectives enhance design, design brings more creativity to roles that are traditionally less creative (such as testing). This boost to creative value is just one of many considerations that will come up as you implement Agile.

8 Implementing Agile: Key Considerations

Embracing Agile entails conforming to a set of working practices across your team. These practices keep the team focused and efficient and foster collaboration. But getting people to approach their work in an Agile fashion will not happen overnight, especially if you're managing an established team. To succeed, you'll need a plan that addresses:

- How you'll leverage internal Agile experts.
- What external training will be required.
- Which method you'll initially adopt.
- When you'll evaluate your initial implementation.

You'll also want to assign a business owner on your team who can dive deeper into key methods such as Scrum and Kanban and manage your team's transformation. (This may be a role you take on personally.) This business lead will be the primary point of contact between your team and others who are leveraging Agile. This individual should also make it clear from the get-go—to your team and to other groups—that an Agile transformation takes time, commitment, and investment. This is why evaluating the initial implementation is so important.

Forging C-Suite Partnerships

Consulting with internal experts, like the CTO or CPO (if your company has them) and their teams is a great place to start. They will have already done some Agile tailoring to fit their method to your company culture. Don't pay attention to the hype that analyst firms have created over the relationship between CMOs and CTOs. Analysts love to harp on the fact that the CMO's budget for technology is growing larger than the CTO's—as if they are stealing this budget from their colleagues! The reality is that Agile is hard, and marketers need to tap into the expertise that CTOs, CIOs, and CPOs have developed. This may mean adopting or even transitioning some talent from their teams, but it does not mean that the CMO won't have to partner with, and rely on, these leaders to achieve his goals. On the contrary, the CTO, CIO, and CPO are critical partners that will become even more important in the future. Remember, success with Agile relies on closer collaboration or cross-functional teams, so be nice to your CTO, CIO, and (or) CPO, and they might help you figure out how to operationalize Agile on your side of the house.

Consider what Mark Saffer, J. Crew's CIO, had to say about his collaboration with marketing:

> Our IT team spends a lot of time with people who run our consumer-facing business [. . . .] This includes style guides, also known as catalogues, that are put together by the marketing department. IT then works with marketing to translate that design and creativity for our website/online platforms.
>
> We use an Agile methodology and spend a lot of time one-on-one and with small groups to understand different needs. The iterative nature of Agile means that we have an ongoing feedback loop and greater reason to collaborate with a broad set of colleagues.[1]

This kind of collaboration is essential. It also reflects how the roles responsible for managing technology are changing within the enterprise (see Figure 2.4). Modernizing the enterprise involves reconfiguring C-suite relationships to best support the business. When it comes to technology management, this means that the CMO and CIO might partner on an internal/external collaboration platform; the CMO and CRO might partner on the sales and marketing automation platform; the CMO and the CPO might partner on an analytics platform; the CTO and the CIO might

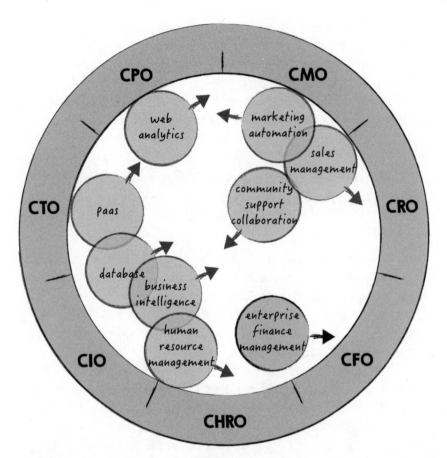

FIGURE 2.4 Technology Management By Role

partner on network infrastructure and storage; and so on. In the end, the CMO is the one whose role is expanding most, because marketers are increasingly being positioned to be the steward of customer experience.

The overall trend is shifting responsibility for technology decisions away from the centralized IT function and toward the line of business. While marketing may be affected the most, this trend will affect the other line of business leaders. One potential benefit of this is increased collaboration between the centralized IT function and the line of business.

"These days, digital transformation is obliterating the line between IT and the business. Business-led IT is huge—and provides a vital source of funding for digital innovation," notes Chris Mixter, senior director of advisory services at the Corporate Executive Board Company (CEB). "When you compare what corporate IT functions spend on innovation and what the business spends on innovation through business-led IT, in absolute dollars [the latter] spend three times as much as we do," Mixter said at the 2014 Oracle CIO Summit. "If you want to hitch your wagon to the horse of innovation, business-led IT is where you go."

C-Suite Technology Collaboration Leads to Innovation: Scenes from Oracle OpenWorld

At Oracle, we see evidence that technology and business innovation have become inextricably part of the same conversation at our biggest conference, Oracle OpenWorld.

Take the attendee list from the 2014 event, for example. The number of marketing chiefs and customer support decision-makers tripled over the 2013 conference, and the number of HR executives and sales leaders nearly doubled. In fact, the CIO of an auto manufacturer said that he'd brought along at least five line-of-business leaders to explore what they could do together to improve the customer experience. "They were a little apprehensive at first. They thought IT people would be walking around spouting acronyms all day. But by the end of the first day, they realized that everything pertained to them as much as it did to IT," he said. That dynamic manifested itself in some interesting ways throughout the proceedings.

Business-Side Speakers and Topics

During one session, executives from three organizations discussed their recent enterprise resource planning (ERP) cloud implementations. Only one was a CIO. The other two were financial executives, and it was clear that they had been closely involved in leading these projects. Indeed, many industry-specific sessions had a similar focus, in which technology lay at the core

(continued)

(continued)

of a business-focused discussion. In one conversation about retail brand differentiation, for example, the CMO of a South American furniture and appliance retailer said that 25 percent of his company's marketing budget went to online projects, and that exploding mobile usage had led his company to accelerate mobile marketing by a full year.

A big-box retailer at the same session emphasized the importance of building a consistent customer experience. His company realized that getting information to the consumer quickly was only the start. The customer experience also had to be the same across multiple channels, whether Twitter, Facebook, or a mobile app. Once again, this clear business requirement came with significant technology implications. The company had to get data from multiple sources into one repository to inform systems running physical stores, online stores, catalogs, and customer service reps.

Interest in Data-Driven Market Opportunities

Data can improve existing products and services, and it can also fuel new business opportunities and solutions. Filippo Passerini, Procter & Gamble's group president, global business services and chief information officer, said that his company works with vendors such as Oracle to create data-driven products and services. "It's an incredible opportunity," he said. The key is to start at the business end rather than the tech side. "It's less about individual technology applications and more about solutions. You have to start with a business model in mind and co-develop, co-create, and go to market with something that works."

Integration as a Business Concern

One of the chief manifestations of the IT-business convergence sits with the evolution of the term *integration* from tech-speak to business priority. A financial executive, for example, said that a primary rationale for her organization's move to cloud-based ERP was the need to jettison legacy applications that didn't speak to each other and that added layers of inefficiency to

(continued)

(continued)

procurement and accounts-payable processes. The automotive CIO, meanwhile, said that after years of integration talk on his part, the business side is now bringing up the topic as part of proposals for new features and functions.

IT's Emergence as Full Business Partner

Most businesses have moved beyond the first step in this process—the alignment of business and technology leaders. Now you have IT and line-of-business partners collaborating on business projects that are jointly conceived and implemented. For example, Intel's IT and marketing groups worked together to expand Intel's marketing strategy with capabilities such as social listening, campaign management, and data management. "It allowed us to amplify our messaging in the marketplace, to know what content people really like and value and push that to the targeted audience," said Kimberly S. Stevenson, Intel's vice president and chief information officer. As a result, the cost of a qualified lead plummeted from $300 to $25 in less than two years. Conversions on those leads improved 75 percent in terms of velocity, while engagement improved by 17 percent.

The Role of the Agile Coach

While internal experts can jump-start your adoption of Agile, not all companies have such experts. Plus, while internal experts can get you started, they cannot own your method. Your team needs to own and tailor its Agile implementation. If the business lead for your implementation is not trained in Agile, you should consider bringing in an expert—an Agile coach. The best possible approach is to have the coach manage a small project with your team and play the role of Scrum Master. After that experience, those team members can train the rest of your team. If you have limited resources you can train a trainer (usually a Scrum Master), but I'd recommend training as many of your active participants as possible.

If you're building a team from scratch, you'll have the benefit of setting expectations right from the start. Leading by example helps, but I can all but guarantee that you'll see some people who just get it out of the gate; they'll love using these practices, and will essentially live in your Agile tool. That might be about 25 percent of your team if you're lucky. The other 75 percent will take time to convert and train, which is why the role of the Scrum master (from the Scrum methodology) can have a big impact on adoption.

At Involver, we brought in an Agile coach to help us establish a more robust Agile practice in development and product management. This benefited my group because marketing and product management had already been working closely together. In fact, the product management team was originally established within the marketing group before it was consolidated with development under our CTO. Our development team had some experience with Agile but our implementation was not rigorous. We had no internal expert or champion, nor did we have an executive mandate to embrace Agile.

That changed when we started work on a product called Conversation Suite. This product was being built to replace an old application that predated my time at the company. The application had a lot of technical debt (the cost associated with fixing poor engineering that results from haste) that was not worth paying off. Suffice it to say that the app had not been built with Agile methods, and certainly not with the rigor of XP. It's not worth deeply analyzing why this happened, but this is a common occurrence at start-ups with younger development teams that are under extreme pressure to ship product. In short, technical debt keeps building up. It's also worth noting that lots of companies that get acquired hold lots of technical debt, so the incentives are not always present to reduce the debt.

In any case, the management team knew that we needed to upgrade our practice. We all felt strongly that we needed to bring in some external expertise to help facilitate an Agile transformation in development. We did this by partnering with Pivotal Labs on the initial development of Conversation Suite. At the time, Pivotal's consultancy model did not support developing applications *for* clients. Rather, they developed applications *with* clients so that those clients could then go forward with an Agile practice of their own. The way that they accomplished this is that they paired a Pivotal developer with an Involver developer for the project (in other words, the XP practice of pair-programming).

Our CTO picked a handful of our most talented developers to participate in the project with the understanding that, once completed, each Involver developer would pair with another Involver developer to share what they'd learned and teach the rest of the team. And that's exactly what happened. In this case, our product owner from product management also participated in the process. Because this role had previously been based in the marketing group, she helped keep marketing working in sync with the development process. She reached out to identify customers to support the process and provide feedback, to align the visual design system from our websites with our service interfaces, and to coordinate communications with the release of each iteration.

Own Your Method

I've never led a strict implementation of any one methodology. Rather, I've introduced methods to my teams and they have worked in collaboration to take elements of each to guide their work. I've also found it immensely helpful to work with Agile consulting firms to help upgrade our practice. At Oracle we even have a services offering designed to help companies implement Agile in the context of our marketing automation offering. Of course, this is all very new to the marketing world, and I suspect that over time, my team—and marketing teams in general—will develop best practices for different types of projects, services, and initiatives.

Agile coaches will likely bring Agile methods to the table when they engage with you. But the best coaches will acknowledge that tailoring the method to your team is critical. In the development context, there is a wealth of best practices to tap into, but at this early point, the marketing world simply hasn't yet had a chance to establish many best practices. That said, as I've talked with marketers, I've observed a familiar pattern: Teams tend to start with a slightly overly prescriptive approach, move to a less prescriptive one, and finally settle somewhere in the middle.

In my experience, more marketing projects fit well with Kanban than with Scrum. This is based on the fact that marketers seem to prefer less prescriptive methods and are less dogmatic about process than developers. It could also be that Kanban is simpler to get started with. Scrum, however, is an excellent fit for things like search engine optimization, online advertising, and marketing automation—activities that are ongoing and that offer a steady stream of feedback.

Set Expectations Up Front

Regardless of the method you choose to start with, feedback on how it's working will be critical to its success. If it's not working, this feedback will enable you to adapt and iterate until you get closer to something that does. The point is, you won't know upfront exactly how long it's going to take to get to a stable process. (See the "The Cone of Uncertainty" that follows.) Thus, it's important to set expectations about this up front.

Set milestones at which you'll conduct reviews of the process to share with your executive partners. If possible, map these reports to the retrospectives associated with each sprint or cycle. Alternatively, you can align reporting to internal adoption goals; at enterprises this is useful when rolling out Agile across many teams. As with all things Agile, the key is to set expectations externally in the same way you operate internally. In other words, respond to feedback and share your progress transparently.

The Cone of Uncertainty

In the Cone of Uncertainty (the graph shown in Figure 2.5), software development guru and author Steve McConnell visualizes what development organizations have learned from experience. At the beginning, it's impossible to know exactly how long a project is going to take or how much investment will be required. The Agile methodology is designed for development in this context—the polar opposite of the Waterfall methodology, which is suited for more certain, stable circumstances.

Marketers and the rest of the business need to understand the reality associated with the Cone of Uncertainty and buy into the approach in order to be successful. Put another way, you're not looking for your colleagues to buy into a service, you're looking for them to buy into a *process* that will lead to a great service.

(continued)

(continued)

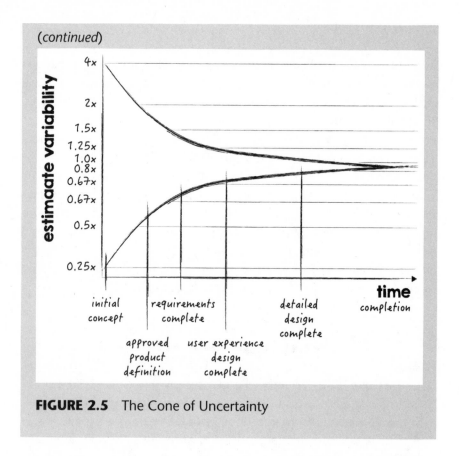

FIGURE 2.5 The Cone of Uncertainty

When thinking about the Cone of Uncertainty, I am reminded of the words of Donald Rumsfeld when being questioned about the Iraq War. He said, "As we know, there are known knowns; there are things we know we know. We also know there are known unknowns; that is to say, we know there are some things we do not know. But there are also unknown unknowns—the ones we don't know we don't know."[2] It's those latter two that require the ability to adapt both tactical implementations and the strategy that drives them.

One of the gaps between the plan and reality stems from the fact that the people who develop a service have expertise that is related to the creation of the services, whereas people who use the service will ultimately have more expertise related to how it works in practice. This is often most apparent when people use a service in ways that the developers did not intend. Sometimes these are seen as hacks, but they are also critical pieces of feedback that can help companies zero in on the right service and move toward the narrow end of the Cone of Uncertainty. One well-known example of this is the use of the "#" or hashtag on Twitter. This hack or linguistic convention allows users to tag tweets with keywords that make searching for tweets on a specific topic easier. Of course, it presented a wonderful opportunity for Twitter to improve its service and it was ultimately integrated into the service.

9

Implementing Agile: Common Objections

Change is hard, especially when you're an incumbent. Change often requires a change maker, and even then there will be pushback. In this chapter, we examine some of the most common arguments against implementing Agile.

Argument #1: "It Doesn't Scale"

Perhaps the most common concern about Agile is the perception that it does not scale well. This is a valid concern, but when put in context I think you'll see that it's not a reason to postpone an Agile implementation.

For product development, Agile methods scale about as well as any other method. The same scale issues that arise with Waterfall tend to come up with Agile. The single biggest one is communication: The more individuals involved in a project, the bigger the challenge it is to ensure good communication. Dunbar's number applies here; it states that there is a limit to the number of people with whom one can maintain stable social relationships. This is, of course, an inherent barrier to scale, not unique to Agile. Collaboration platforms such as Asana can help increase the number of relationships an individual can maintain. Like social networks, they facilitate communication and provide a record of relationships, conversations, projects, and documents in the cloud—but there are still limits.

Scaling anything is hard when humans are involved. Agile, however, includes practices that improve our ability to collaborate at scale. For example, in the engineering context, XP's focus on granular functionality, along with its shared coding practices, makes it easier for any developer to understand and validate the functionality of code written by anyone else. The key here is having a shared discipline and shared communication practices. Marketing could augment scale, too, following that same basic approach: codifying ways of working, such as establishing annotation standards, brand standards, and workflows; using analytics; and so forth. Plus, by its very nature, Agile tends to nudge its users to find ways to break down—and scale down—initiatives to the minimum required for each iteration. So it naturally limits scope creep, which, in turn, reduces scaling issues.

Argument #2: "We'll Disrupt Active Projects"

This may be the easiest objection to overcome, if only because you can't possibly transition all projects to an Agile process overnight! Instead, it's best to start with a project that allows your team to learn the process while tailoring it to your company culture. Once you've got an Agile team up and running, it's much easier to spin off an individual who can start the next team when a new project arises.

As you proceed, it's essential to measure performance so that you can compare the productivity of your Agile teams to that of your traditional teams. At some point, you'll be able to determine whether Agile is resulting in better performance. And by the time you're ready to craft the business case to support a switch, you'll have the experience required to do so.

Is Agile Really Faster?

Yes and no. Fundamentally, people can only get so much done in a day. Will Agile help people get more done in a day than Waterfall? No. If, however, you reframe the question as "What does Agile
(continued)

(continued)

accelerate?," then you can definitely identify certain types of initiatives that it can speed up. Certainly, Agile gets you to an initial iteration or an initial release faster. In that way, Agile also gets you to feedback faster and typically gets you to a product/market fit faster. This is why Agile is so popular among start-ups.

For projects that are highly predictable, the Waterfall approach lets you optimize them more fully. In other words, Waterfall has the potential to be faster as long as the plan doesn't veer from the final destination. Agile, on the other hand, gives up some speed in exchange for increasing the likelihood that you'll end up at the right destination; it improves your ability to steer and change course. If Waterfall leads to the wrong outcome, its speed advantage disappears. So Waterfall is riskier in quickly evolving industries.

Argument #3: "We Can't Plan Ahead"

Embracing Agile makes it impossible to tell your colleagues exactly where you'll be directing your team over the coming year. Your plan is an antiplan—an alternative to developing an annual marketing plan. It respects the three simple truths about development we cited earlier:

1. It is impossible to gather all the requirements at the beginning of a project.
2. Whatever requirements you do gather are guaranteed to change.
3. There will always be more to do than time and money will allow.[1]

In other words, it's impossible to forecast exactly what you'll do (see Figure 2.6).

Indeed, marketers are struggling to establish realistic plans in the face of an ever-increasing rate of innovation. A recent Forrester Research study found that 96 percent of marketers agreed or strongly agreed with the statement, "The pace of change in technology and marketing will continue to accelerate." In addition, the study determined that "The traditional annual

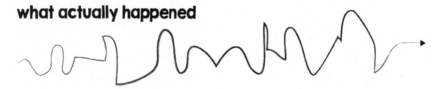

FIGURE 2.6 The Truth About Plans

planning routine is ripe for extinction, as 69 percent of our B2B marketing leaders say that conditions change too quickly to keep plans current."[2]

Argument #4: "How Can We Possibly Budget for This?"

Marketers need to adjust the way they work to accommodate, reflect, and support changes in development. As marketing embraces Agile and the approach gains momentum across the company, it will eventually impact finance. Without an annual plan, it's just not possible to produce a reliable annual budget projection.

That's not to say that Agile teams can't manage to a budget; they can, and do. The problem is that doing so promotes behaviors that are inconsistent with the Agile approach. Bjarte Bogsnes, vice president of performance management development at Statoil, the Norwegian oil giant, sums it up nicely: "Handing out bags of money each year might seem an effective way of capping such costs, especially if managers are reminded of the consequences of overspending. The problem is that setting a ceiling also sets a floor; managers know that not spending their budget is not smart if they want to ensure the same level of resources next year."[3] This practically guarantees that resources are not going to be allocated efficiently. Without being able to adapt and reallocate funds at mid-year, one team might have to slow down for lack of resources while another sits on a pile of cash (or spends it on something that does not maximize ROI).

Bjarte is a leading thinker in the Beyond Budgeting Movement, which essentially injects Agile into the discipline of financial management. He points out that "Forecasting is actually a way of compensating for lack of agility."[4] In reality, it is much more efficient and effective to engage with teams, just as a bank does, so finance engages with teams that require more budget when the need actually arises. This allows finance to scrutinize each investment more closely when the inputs being considered are fresh and most relevant.

I am not aware of a single marketing team that manages its budget with a dynamic process like Bjarte's, but this is not a hard requirement for Agile. Agile can work under strict budget constraints, but given a dynamic budget process I believe it would thrive.

10

Your North Star: The Agile Marketing Manifesto

O kay, so you've selected a method, appointed an Agile leader, trained your team, overcome objections, and you're ready to take on your first official Agile project. The training wheels are about to come off. It would be handy to have a point on the horizon to track your progress. It turns out that some very smart marketers have collaborated on a marketing-centric interpretation of the Agile Manifesto to help do just that.

Your Team's North Star

There have been many attempts to articulate a set of Agile principles for marketers. The website http://agilemarketingmanifesto.org/ offers the best (consolidated) version that I've come across so far. Like the Agile Manifesto, it includes both values and principles. Here are the values:

- Validated learning over opinions and conventions
- Customer-focused collaboration over silos and hierarchy
- Adaptive and iterative campaigns over Big-Bang campaigns
- The process of customer discovery over static prediction
- Flexible versus rigid planning
- Responding to change over following a plan
- Many small experiments over a few large bets

And here are the principles:

- Our highest priority is to satisfy the customer through early and continuous delivery of marketing that solves problems.
- We welcome and plan for change. We believe that our ability to quickly respond to change is a source of competitive advantage.
- Deliver marketing programs frequently, from a couple of weeks to a couple of months, with a preference to the shorter timescale.
- Great marketing requires close alignment with the business people, sales, and development.
- Build marketing programs around motivated individuals. Give them the environment and support they need, and trust them to get the job done.
- Learning, through the build-measure-learn feedback loop, is the primary measure of progress.
- Sustainable marketing requires you to keep a constant pace and pipeline.
- Don't be afraid to fail; just don't fail the same way twice.
- Continuous attention to marketing fundamentals and good design enhances agility.
- Simplicity is essential.[1]

It's worth flipping back to Chapter 4 to compare this interpretation to the original Agile Manifesto. By now, the original should make much more sense. I hope that this marketing-centric interpretation becomes more and more resonant as you continue reading. I strongly recommend pinning the Agile Marketing Manifesto on your wall in a conspicuous place as you start putting Agile to work for your business.

A Complementary Design Metaphor

As I've said before, Agile can be baked into almost any type of product or service development project. My former colleague from Adaptive Path, Brandon Schauer, likes to tell a story about The Cupcake Model of product strategy that is relevant here.

Traditional businesses can think of their product or service as a cake. There are three basic parts to the cake:

1. The cake. This is the main substance of the offering; think of it as the structure that supports the product or service.
2. The filling. This sits between the layers of cake and makes it tasty; think of it as the features that make up the product or service.
3. The icing. This is what makes the cake look so impressive; think of it as the front-end experience that customers interface with.

This metaphor might remind you of the Waterfall approach, because there, too, you have to make the cake first, then add the filling, and finally add the icing. But how might our product look from a more adaptive perspective? Let's think of our product as a cupcake. A cupcake has everything that a cake has: it's got cake, filling, and icing. But cupcakes are much smaller and therefore easier to make.

By making cupcakes, you can test how much people like them before committing to the full-size cake—thus adhering to the Agile Marketing Manifesto's first value (Validated learning over opinions and conventions) and second value (Customer-focused collaboration over silos and hierarchy). In fact, you can afford to experiment and create many cupcakes for what it would cost to make a full-size cake. The fact is that you won't know up front which cupcakes are worth turning into cake (Value 6: Responding to change over following a plan). You might make cupcakes in different shapes, for example, or you might put the cupcake on a stick like a popsicle. You'll have many more opportunities to test out your fillings and icings. In short, you'll be able to put something out there quickly and get feedback quickly (Value 4: The process of customer discovery over static prediction, and 5: Flexible versus rigid planning). If you're familiar with Eric Reis's popular book *The Lean Startup* this should sound familiar. Reis talks about leveraging early adopters (who help validate product/market fit) to help bring your product or service to market as you iterate on it (Value 3: Adaptive and iterative campaigns over Big-Bang campaigns).

What you are putting out may be a prototype, or a minimum viable product (MVP), in Lean parlance. As Reis explains in a 2009 blog post: "The minimum viable product is that version of a new product which allows a team to collect the maximum amount of validated learning about customers with the least effort."[2] In many cases, you do not have to build the actual product to validate its value with the market. Instead, it is possible to build a lightweight prototype or proxy that can be used to achieve the same end. This is something that marketers should be very used to and comfortable with because it complements existing market research practices. With this example in mind, try a thought experiment by replacing "cake" with "website" and "cupcake" with "web page."

As for applying Agile to a website, the cupcake in that case might be the redesign of a single page or section of the site, a landing page or perhaps even the home page. Following this approach you might create a few versions of the page or section and conduct A/B testing to understand which performs best. What you learn from this small-scale experience can dramatically impact and inform the larger investment that is yet to come.

Repurposing Content Cupcakes

Adopting the cupcake approach has a side benefit: Often, it will support adjacent objectives. Say you created an application programming interface (API) that makes data from one system accessible to another. That same API (or API structure) could be repurposed to integrate other technologies. Moreover, the cupcake concept isn't limited to technology, platforms, and services. Consider content cupcakes. Imagine releasing a book chapter by chapter to a small audience and then later releasing a definitive consolidated version that incorporates the feedback that you've received along the way (that's essentially what I've done with this book).

One advantage of this approach is that it provides content in a scalable fashion to support content-hungry programs like marketing automation and social marketing. Before your book was even published, you could start leveraging the cupcakes from which it was made. By slicing and dicing the book you could support content requirements for your website, webinar programs, retail experience, social program, and more (see Figure 2.7). Not to mention that you'll get feedback on those smaller components, which will help you improve the consolidated version over time.

As you move from cupcakes to cake, you'll discover why the era of developing one-off investments, campaigns, and projects is largely over. This is stated plainly in the Agile Marketing Manifesto with Values 3 and

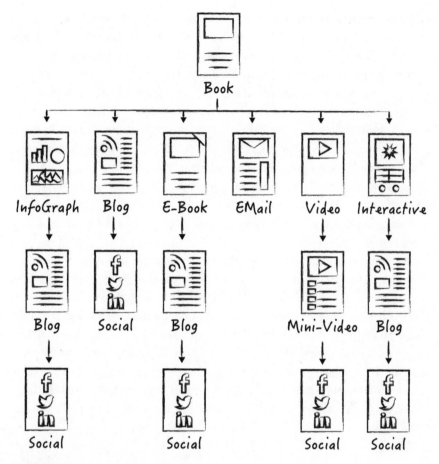

FIGURE 2.7 Content Flow

7 (Adaptive and iterative campaigns over Big-Bang campaigns and Many small experiments over a few large bets). It makes more sense to start baking cupcakes that are released incrementally and that consolidate into larger releases and integrations.

Going Cupcake Crazy

As we've discussed, marketers today are confronting major challenges when it comes to establishing an integrated marketing platform (a really big cake). They've got discrete technologies for managing their many programs: the websites, digital experiences, mobile apps, e-mail fulfillment, marketing automation, CRM and customer databases, social channels, community and support platforms, content development, analytics—the list goes on.

Any complete platform will include owned services as well as acquired services that will need to be integrated. You'll probably have to build an internal tech team but you'll also have to rely on external partners for some tasks. To support web personalization, each implementation will require some amount of development, from the front-end configuration of your CRM to the back-end development of your website. In short, marketers are looking at a lot of development work, which explains the refrains from analysts that CMOs will soon outspend their CTOs on technology. Suffice it to say, it's easy to get overwhelmed. But wait—don't start with the cake! Start with a cupcake!

Yes, modern marketers are building a platform to deliver marketing-as-a-service (MaaS). Yes, doing so will require restructuring your organization, including establishing a marketing-centric tech team. And yes, this will go beyond just marketing systems to encompass all the content that fuels marketing automation. Begin with your MVP, your cupcake: an anchor experience that is essential, fundamental, and critical to your success, and then start the wheels of Agile turning. Once you've chosen your method, gotten your team rolling with the process, and have demonstrated the benefit of an Agile approach, you'll begin to see meaningful progress toward integration.

Linking Innovation and Customer Experience

11

Integrating Marketing and Innovation with Agile

When the innovation team and the marketing team are aligned through their common use of Agile, customers' experience—from their very first steps in the buyer's journey to their ongoing experience of the product or service—can feel utterly consistent, as though driven by the same source. And, as we'll see in upcoming chapters, alignment does more than enable a coherent experience for the customer; it opens up a whole array of new marketing opportunities that were previously not accessible.

Sharing practices enables different groups to speak the same language. Agile thus serves as a platform for strategic alignment. But Agile isn't the be-all and end-all. Some marketing and innovation methods cannot be aligned within the context of Agile. In fact, there are a number of traditional research and strategy practices that exist outside of the Agile approach— notably, long-term planning—but that must be reconciled with Agile. In this chapter, we'll explore several dimensions of Agile alignment, as well as how to reconcile the kinds of feedback that don't fit with the Agile approach.

Aligning Teams

Thus far we've discussed the basic alignment of groups and processes that comes from using Agile as a common practice. And we've explored the ways in which marketers need to update their practices and platforms in order to enable alignment. But alignment isn't a one-way street; it's not just a matter of how marketing syncs with innovation. Not to mix metaphors, but it takes two to tango. The innovation side needs to do its part.

Alignment is indisputably the goal. But in reality, it is the exception and not the rule.

Why is misalignment so prevalent? The answer lies partly in the evolution of the product management's organizational home. At the beginning of the broadcast era, product management often reported to marketing. Product management (and sometimes product development, too) was often referred to as inbound marketing, while outbound marketing referred to the product marketing function. More recently, particularly at technology companies, product management was established alongside product development—or shifted there—to report to the CTO. And company size has an influence in where product management sits as well; smaller companies tend to give product management more autonomy.

Today, bigger companies are following the approach that smaller companies have established: They're transitioning product management to the C-suite level, equivalent to the level from which marketing is managed. This is preferable—and appropriate—for the area that is the primary driver of innovation. And although product management adopted Agile during its time within the development group, it now needs the autonomy to develop its own Agile method, one that is distinct from development's.

Why? Because it must serve the needs of the user experience (UX) design function situated within product management. Sadly, product management UX design is often under-resourced (although that is changing as product management solidifies its position at the C-suite level). Following this, product management is increasingly becoming a hub that works with development on implementation and with marketing on strategy, research, and go-to-market activities. Recalling the principles of the Agile Manifesto, there is an emphasis on cross-functional teams. Thus product management's Agile team should welcome participation from development and marketing. This might mean that marketers stand in with these teams to facilitate alignment. Alternatively, it can mean that the business leads from each Agile team sync up on a regular cadence. Similarly, product management should be welcome to join marketing's Agile team, and development should be invited to stand in occasionally to drive complete alignment as well. The key is to have cross-functional teams in each business unit and to have cross-functional participation across business units to ensure that the Agile teams stay in sync.

Some groups will synchronize their sprints to support alignment, but this is not a requirement for most companies. There will always be some need to overcome the differences between each Agile implementation. This shouldn't be hard if everyone is speaking the language of Agile. So having adequate overlap at the practice level helps ensure that each team understands the other's interpretation of Agile. As you'd expect, development and product management typically connect on user stories, interaction design, user experience, estimates, and velocity. In aligning with marketing, development and product management will focus on the shared vision of brand (and/or product) as well as on positioning, competitive differentiation, and on the overarching design system and user experience. Few companies are aligned in this fashion today, but this approach will likely take hold as Agile is adopted more widely across organizations.

Aligning UX

Even in those organizations that have invested in modernizing their marketing approach—establishing a full-fledged UX team in product management—there is still often a disconnect between product management's UX design team and marketing's UX design team. This disconnect undermines the company's ability to deliver a consistent user experience.

What a waste. Here are two design groups made up of people with the same job descriptions and the same skills. They inherently speak the same language and share many practices. Yet at most companies, they have little to do with each other. Connecting the two can be a powerful lever for breaking down silos within the enterprise—and advancing marketers' progress in embedding some of their programs directly into the product or service.

Establishing an Agile UX design team within product management and then connecting that team with the UX function on the marketing side is a requirement for a successful Agile transformation—and a critical element of modernizing marketing.

Though I did not know it at the time, my experience at Adaptive Path led me to this realization. Adaptive Path helped forge a new approach to product strategy and design that was adaptive and Agile. In fact, it was ahead of its time in incorporating Agile into product management (a practice also known as *design thinking*). The company taught its clients the importance of validating product strategy before actually building the product. This mind-set, very much in line with Agile, involves leveraging a variety of lightweight or low-fidelity prototyping techniques (such as paper proto-types and wireframes) to validate direction. From there, it's possible to move toward higher fidelity prototypes (such as mock-ups that include visual or even interaction design) to support iterative development. Innovation in prototyping has exploded in the last few years, and Agile design techniques could fill a book of their own.

The point here is not *how* your team chooses to prototype, but rather *that* it uses prototypes to test innovative product ideas and marketing concepts. Obviously the tools you choose will depend on the type of service that you're prototyping, but if you choose well, you will be able to transition smoothly from prototyping to production to promotion. While product management will drive the prototype-creation process (for initiatives related to the core product or service), marketing can help generate product ideas and concepts. And it can also help present those prototypes to representative users in the customer base. When it comes to marketing-oriented initiatives, marketing may drive the process with support from product management.

Aligning the Teams on Research and Feedback

The product innovations that your company identifies must be validated against direct customer feedback and market research. Although Agile meth-ods lead to innovative ideas, defining the product strategy, including the go-to-market strategy, calls for a more holistic approach, especially given the wider range of inputs. It's a mistake to think that one approach is enough for innovation. Agile methods are not optimized to accept the full range of feedback. And traditional research methods are simply out of sync with Agile product development practices, chiefly because Agile development and product management move much faster than traditional marketing research.

To illustrate, compare the inputs that come from the direct consumers of a service with those from the people who manage the consumers of the service (so, practitioner feedback to business feedback or consumer feedback to retailer feedback). Direct-user feedback is constant, whereas

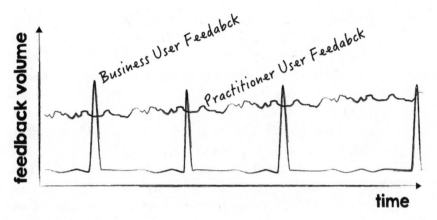

FIGURE 3.1   Feedback Cadences Compared

business feedback is intermittent, typically captured in customer meetings or through customer advisory boards that meet quarterly or less frequently (see Figure 3.1).

In a software context, feedback is characterized differently insofar as practitioners are typically focused on day-to-day objectives (such as updating websites, developing messaging, and maintaining social channels), whereas business leaders are thinking further out. Because Agile is adapted to the practitioners' perspective, it tends to miss broader strategic changes in the landscape. Said another way, the practitioners are in the trenches and the business leaders are looking down from 10,000 feet. Integrating these two perspectives in a compelling, measurable, and responsive fashion is a challenge.

Many companies run into trouble by focusing only on direct customer feedback. Take those companies that developed Facebook applications that lived on Facebook.com brand pages. At Involver, we competed with many such companies, some of which devoted far more attention to this means of gleaning direct customer feedback than we did. They innovated more than we did on these apps, but many of these companies would have been better off putting more effort into scenario planning. Had they done so, they might have picked up on signals from the market (and from Facebook directly) that brand-page apps were not long for this world. Instead they innovated right off a cliff that they never saw coming. Meanwhile, Involver developed a more diversified portfolio of services that mitigated risk and insulated us from this change in direction at Facebook.

The mechanisms for digesting the different types of feedback may be different, but the feedback flows must periodically intersect in order to align implementation with strategy. This process of reconciliation involves comparing and contrasting feedback from each source. Generally, this process raises questions that require further research to validate or resolve. From this reconciliation process, strategic insights emerge.

When it comes to market research, marketers have considerably more expertise than product managers. But product managers move fast; they need answers now, and often the feedback they need comes directly from the systems they're building. Still, relying only on that ground-level view can spell trouble, as Involver's competitors' Facebook experience shows. Granted, we marketers need to evolve our methods to more effectively support Agile (and faster iteration cycles). But marketers are in a position to lead the collaboration required to get there. In some cases, this will mean training product management on how to do lightweight DIY research. In more complex cases, marketers will apply Agile research methods to support product management.

Aligning on Strategy

The high-frequency feedback that drives iteration is actually inconsistent with the concept of strategy. As Values 4, 5, and 6 of the Agile Marketing Manifesto—the process of customer discovery over static prediction, flexible versus rigid planning, and responding to change over following a plan—it's not about having a strategy or plan, rather it's about responding to feedback.

But that in no way means that strategy is no longer relevant. No organization can survive without a clear position on how and what it will compete on, without a blueprint that's grounded in an assessment of the market environment, its internal capabilities, its differentiation, and so on. A ground-level view has its place, but when it's the only view, the organization becomes myopic; it can't see the forest for the trees. Similarly, companies that focus on the long-term or 10,000-foot view while ignoring fast-changing market and customer dynamics will be left behind to wonder what happened.

Research, feedback, and strategy are intimately intertwined, and the fact that these inputs come in through different channels at different cadences creates reconciliation challenges. Agile serves the immediate reality, while strategy looks further out. But the two must be reconciled: strategy with the inputs of immediate feedback, Agile with the more macro considerations of strategy. Otherwise, the business will be left in competitors' dust, and Agile teams will suffer the fate of lemmings.

Strategy practices such as scenario planning, which explores how you might respond (or adapt) to potential changes in the landscape, don't fit neatly into an Agile framework. Scenario planning, which is inherently based on future possibility, is not meant to identify the single most likely scenario. Rather, it is designed to help management conceive a broad range of scenarios (and their ramifications) so that they can better anticipate and, when the time comes, respond more quickly to market changes. Similarly, experience mapping, which maps a customer's journey across all touchpoints, can require time-consuming research and a significant investment. Experience mapping yields insights for product or service enhancement, but it, too, does not fit directly into an Agile framework.

As the team that knows what can (and can't) be built, product management is, in a very practical sense, the manager—or better yet, the steward—of product strategy. Scenario planning should be led by product management. But it cannot be done effectively without closely collaborating with marketing. As the team that knows what customers go through—on the website, in retail locations, and at every other touchpoint—marketing is effectively the steward of the overall customer experience. Experience mapping is marketing's bailiwick. Here again, close collaboration with product management is critical, especially when it comes to the experience in the product or service. More broadly, this is the case with any touchpoint that references the experience in the product or service.

If there is no clear link between strategy and the overall customer experience (that is, from the buyer's journey through customer support), problems arise. Product strategy and customer experience must be developed collaboratively if they are to be optimally effective. Such coordination is what makes it possible for marketers to bake marketing into the product itself.

12

Beyond Agile: More Methods to Link Marketing and Product Management with Innovation

I hope that by now I've convinced you that to be a modern marketer you'll need to embrace Agile. Marketers, however, cannot rely exclusively on Agile for managing their work. Instead, we must integrate Agile methods with more traditional methodologies that support a broader range of practice. In this chapter, we'll look at two innovation methods that are representative of the critical practices that do not fit into Agile methods but that must be reconciled with Agile. I also offer a strategy exercise designed to help promote greater strategic alignment between marketing and product management.

And by the way, marketing isn't the only organization that must employ traditional methods. Product management must, as well. That's because marketing and product management share a broader scope of practice than all other organizations, and that is inherently strategic. Moreover, they must align holistically to lead the business together. As Peter Drucker observed, these two groups are distinguished as the sole drivers of the business.

> Because the purpose of business is to create a customer, the business enterprise has two—and only two—basic functions: marketing and innovation. Marketing and innovation produce results; all the rest are costs.[1]

Development can rely more exclusively on Agile because it is more focused on implementation and reaction to immediate feedback than planning. In fact, trying to predict the future (i.e., longer term strategy) runs counter to the Agile Manifesto's fourth value: responding to change over following a plan. But this value is also an inherent limitation of Agile, in that it holds what is at times a myopic view of planning and strategy. There is a subtle difference between following a plan and having a strategy practice that informs Agile. In the latter case, strategic planning takes place outside of your Agile practice and produces insights that may ultimately have to be addressed by the Agile team. In this way, a strategic planning practice does not fundamentally contradict Agile.

As I'll point out with the strategy exercise that follows, strategic planning is as much about strengthening your ability to react to change (through the process of playing out a range of possible scenarios) as it is about committing to any particular scenario. From this perspective, a strategy practice is about training for success and mitigating risk. It's also worth noting that following a plan at the implementation level has very different implications than following a plan at the business level. Understanding macro trends at the business level is not only possible, it is necessary. It's extremely tough to predict specific market changes, but it's entirely possible to recognize broader, longer term trends.

We've explored how Agile can serve as a platform for alignment between marketing and innovation teams. But it can also extend these teams' ability to align in other, more extensive, ways. Teams that are aligned through Agile are, for example, better able to align on innovation methods and strategy practices that exist outside of the Agile approach. Today, this is still the exception rather than the norm.

According to a 2013 report by Forrester Research, CMOs and CIOs lack established practices that put them on the same page with respect to strategy. While this research concerns CIOs and not CPOs, I believe that for the sake of this argument the CIO is a reasonable proxy, because this person supports product management and collaborates closely with the CTO and CPO in managing technology.

Our 2013 survey results showed that the marketing technology strategy map is not yet understood by the organization. For collaboration to work, CMOs and CIOs must jointly define the roadmap to guide their teams in the same direction. CMOs and CIOs need to move beyond territorial ownership to build a joint IT —from mastering the data flow to identifying customer insights that power decisions and drive sales.[2]

More recent Forrester research from 2014 indicates that things are moving in the right direction when it comes to communication.

The survey results indicate that CMOs and CIOs are making strides to improve their communication with each other. Seventy percent of tech management leaders and 59 percent of marketing leaders agree that their CMO and CIO now meet regularly to review objectives and priorities, up by 9 and 14 percentage points, respectively, from last year.

But the report also states:

On the flip side, one of the disappointments in this year's survey has been virtually no progress in solving the problems that CMOs and CIOs face in turning large amounts of data into actionable customer insights.[3]

So, communication is the first step but not a solution. What's needed are methods and practices that go beyond communication to action. As Drucker proclaimed more than 30 years ago, the marketing organization and the product management organization need to own these foundational practices jointly to deliver results. Let's first explore collaboration on the innovation side, where opportunities for better communication and collaboration abound.

Common Innovation Methods

Entire books have been written on the topic of innovation methods, so I won't attempt to provide a comprehensive overview here. As you'd expect, each method has its pros and cons. A diversified approach to innovation will therefore deliver more consistent results, and is likelier to produce a return on investment. I will share two general methods to establish the range of what's possible. I'll then highlight the need for alignment. In both cases, the innovative ideas derived from these methods must ultimately be reconciled with your Agile practice. (Note that we'll explore methods and not specific practices, such as scenario planning, which could be incorporated into either method.)

Skunk Works

Skunk Works is the official alias for Lockheed Martin's Advanced Development Program, a special R&D group established in the 1940s. Today the term is used to refer to any dedicated innovation team that operates outside of the procedural strictures of a company. A skunk works is granted relative autonomy from a company's normal business practices and constraints in order to accelerate innovation, usually of a specific project, and usually (though not necessarily) in secret. A skunk works team can be composed of key players from product management or outsiders. The skunk works approach is often a good fit for organizations that have not yet adopted Agile. By isolating this innovation team and freeing it from the constraints of conventional practices and standard company procedures, it can embrace Agile without hindrance from the predominant corporate culture.

Google X Labs is a good example of a modern skunk works, with its firewall dividing it from Google's mainstream business. A kind of mega-skunk works, Google X is developing more than 100 very different moon shot ideas, including self-driving cars, wearable computers, and new wind-energy systems. Many other major companies are taking a similar approach to innovation, among them Nike, Walmart, Nordstrom, and Xerox.

Crowdsourcing

This increasingly (and literally) popular approach appears to be the polar opposite of skunk works, because it characteristically opens up the innovation process to the general public. "My Starbucks Idea" allows customers to propose product improvements and vote on submitted ideas; the most popular ones get implemented. Through the Netflix Prize, a developer contest, independent engineers design an improved movie recommendation engine. Advocacy and peer-to-peer support communities, such as the Oracle ACE

Program, give a company's most influential users a platform through which to shape product innovation.

Crowdsourcing is generally understood as a way of extending innovation to your entire community. But it can also be an internal-only process that allows anyone within your company to submit and develop ideas for innovation.

With skunk works, the stand-alone team might prototype and validate ideas for the primary product management organization to actually build. In the skunk works examples just cited, teams are doing more than just coming up with ideas for innovation; they are implementing those ideas. Crowdsourcing, although seemingly only about generating the ideas, can also entail building the ideas. At Netflix, the engineers actually developed the algorithm that was to be integrated into the site.

Going one step further, it's not hard to imagine how a skunk works team might tackle crowdsourced ideas, or conversely, how a company might crowdsource innovation based on ideas developed by a skunk works team. These methods are not mutually exclusive. They organize teams and resources in unique ways, but each requires alignment between marketing and innovation in order to be successful. In the case of skunk works, marketing can support the effort with everything from market research to branding, and research subjects. With crowdsourcing, marketers can leverage their existing web and community platforms to facilitate the crowdsourcing process. Incidentally, the community platforms that marketers manage can serve both internal and external communities. Further, they can serve as a bridge between these communities to facilitate feedback and collaboration in the service of ideation.

My Starbucks Idea is a great example of a program that thrives on alignment while spinning off value on an ongoing basis. Is this an innovation site, a customer support site, an employee feedback site, or a marketing site? It's all of the above. Yes, it generates and qualifies ideas that product management can take on. Yes, many ideas attempt to resolve customer complaints or issues. Yes, launching each idea presents marketing with an opportunity to simultaneously celebrate a new release and a community member. Marketing would not promote this site if product management were not committed to implementing the ideas it generates. That's a form of alignment that can be extended.

And, by the way, My Starbucks Idea is also a community platform for conducting the research that will inform both marketing and product management on which ideas have the greatest potential. In other words, these two groups are both vested in this site, and it focuses their respective attention on the same ideation process and top ideas.

So, with marketing and product management united in the effort to developing a funnel of innovative ideas, how can they align on the strategy to implement them?

Top-Down Strategy

Following are two strategy exercises designed to help foster alignment between marketing and product management. These exercises support strategy by showing the dependencies between and among initiatives and by defining how these initiatives should be prioritized—that is, in which order they should be carried out. Like the Kanban board, the power of these exercises lies partly in the way they help users visualize strategy. (By the way, these exercises are also useful for planning sprints.)

Remember: The key to developing a solid product strategy is understanding that resources define the constraint to what can be accomplished. Developing a viable strategy always involves making hard choices about how to allocate limited resources over time. The most effective strategies are those that elicit more no's than yese's from leaders. In other words, although there are usually many options that you could pursue, a good strategy dictates that there are only a few that you will actually pursue.

Dependency Exercise

This exercise represents the innovative ideas that you've developed as potential initiatives. It gets marketing and product management leaders to define the interdependencies that exist between initiatives. For example, if Tesla wants car owners to be able to summon their cars from the garage using the mobile app, the company must first enable self-driving, mobile connectivity, and a range of other capabilities that might have stand-alone value. The list of initiatives is essentially a high-level backlog of stories that themselves could be broken down into backlogs of their own during the development process. (In the development context, the high-level lists are sometimes referred to as *epics*, which are made up of a series of associated

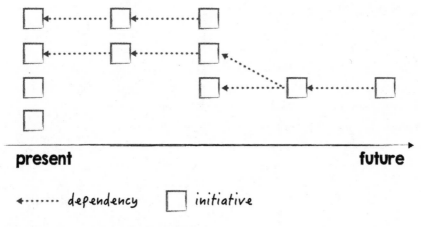

FIGURE 3.2 Dependency Map

stories.) Note that each initiative should have some stand-alone value of its own. Thus, if a dependency has no stand-alone value, it should be incorporated directly into the initiative it supports.

Once you've collected your list of initiatives (or epics), you'll identify any overlap and consolidate where possible. Remember, you are not committing to carrying out all of these initiatives; you're simply organizing them to better understand how they relate to each other (see Figure 3.2).

This is done by plotting the initiatives on a timeline (you needn't write in actual dates). Dependencies must be placed earlier on the timeline than the initiatives that they support. Dependencies are represented by lines between the initiatives. Note that some initiatives will have multiple dependencies and some will share dependencies.

Prioritization Exercise

This exercise helps you visualize which initiatives should be prioritized based on their feasibility and importance, in effect, which ones will yield the greatest return on investment. Start by listing the set of initiatives that you want to prioritize (this may not be everything on your timeline) in the left-hand column of the table (as in Figure 3.3). It is best to start with the list of items that do not have dependencies, otherwise you might prioritize an initiative above its dependency. If you do want to include items with

initiative	feasability	importance
1	6	1
2	2	3
3	1	4
4	6	5
5	5	6
6	6	8
7	9	8
total	7 x 5 = 35	7 x 5 = 35

FIGURE 3.3 Prioritization Table & Graph

dependencies, it's best to consolidate the initiative and its dependencies as one item on your list.

Then, assign each initiative a feasibility and importance rating. Typically, product management assigns the feasibility values with support from development; they know whether the idea can be built and what it would take. The "importance" column represents ratings that marketing and product management agree on.

The values you assign to each of the two criteria are based on a total budget of points. Figure 3.3 shows seven potential initiatives; note that I've allotted a total budget of 35 points. You can set any total budget; the more you allot, the higher fidelity the results will be. So, if I allotted budget evenly across the initiatives in Figure 3.3, each would have 5 points (35 points divided by 7 equals 5 points). Of course, you would never distribute points evenly because the whole point is to show relative importance and feasibility. Remember, if you consolidate an initiative (to include a dependency) you must factor it into the cost of the initiative; so if the primary initiative costs 10 points and its dependency initiative costs 2, you must assign 12 points to its feasibility rating.

Once you've plugged ratings into the table, you then plot the initiatives' values on the chart to the right. This allows you to plot them within three priority zones. Those closest to the top-right corner—the highest priority initiatives—have the greatest ROI.

That said, the items represented in the top right do not constitute a strategy that you commit to. Nor am I suggesting that you shouldn't carry out initiatives that fall below the top zone. But this exercise will give both organizations a much better shared understanding of the initiatives and how they relate to each other. With these insights in hand, they'll be better equipped to articulate a strategy that both product development and marketing can own and support.

In this exercise, it's useful to have each participant come up with his or her own rating of feasibility or importance before sharing with the team. By concealing the results in this way, you avoid introducing the form of cognitive bias known as *anchoring*, in which the first number spoken aloud sets a precedent for subsequent estimates. You can then average all the individual ratings and rebalance them against your total budget. I've done this using a shared spreadsheet that averages everyone's inputs into a master sheet.

Sometimes it makes sense to divide each of the feasibility and importance columns into two columns that you average together: "technical feasibility" and "creative feasibility" and "importance to the user" and "importance to the business." For this approach, simply combine those two columns to come up with a total budget allocation.[4]

As a final step, you might revisit the first exercise and update it based on the results from the second. The second time around, the feasibility scores make it possible to loosely define dates (though with what we know about the cone of uncertainty, you should not rely on these estimates). The sequence that you define is, in effect, the foundation for the narrative of your strategy. Doing so will also help you pinpoint dependencies and other potential interactions between initiatives that you may have overlooked. Finally, it is also a great way to play out alternative scenarios.

This articulated strategy then becomes a North Star (or a constellation of stars) that Agile teams can use to validate they're not iterating too far off course. This document should not be treated as a static articulation, because it will quickly prove fragile. Rather, the document embodies strategic insights and values to guide interpretation on an ongoing basis. It's also much faster to update this document than it is to create it from scratch, a process that is worth doing at least quarterly.

This approach gels with what Forrester has found in its research:

> To [achieve alignment], CIOs and CMOs need to meet at least twice per month, with the intent of those meetings being to manage the pace of change across the two departments and identify communication gaps. The agile teams should be meeting daily or nearly daily to keep the pace up. Put guardrails in place that clarify acceptable

project scope, cost, and business impact to keep projects manageable and relevant, limiting projects to those that map to corporate or divisional growth projections or those with a business case that can prove a margin-positive return on investment within a two-year time frame.[5]

Putting It All Together

Is it really marketing's job to support product management in diversifying its innovation practice? Is it product management's job to understand the overall customer experience from presales to support? The answer to both questions is "yes."

The structure of the human brain provides a good metaphor for conceiving how marketing and product management should function together. The human brain contains overlapping and partially redundant systems; take, for example, the rods and cones in the vision system. If you removed one or the other, humans would still be able to see, although with diminished ability in many circumstances (e.g., low-light situations). Further, behind the actual receptors are a number of parallel systems for interpreting incoming data. Some serve to recognize and interpret faces, while others interpret the boundaries between objects. In much the same way, marketing and product management should complement each other. In companies, as in biological evolution, overlapping systems have proven to be valuable, and well worth some additional overhead expense associated with maintaining some redundancy.

For marketing, it's not a question of whether to do this work; it's a question of recognizing the unique value that marketing has to offer in various circumstances. While marketing establishes the platform that supports the collection of practitioner feedback, it traditionally has stronger capabilities on the strategic side. When it comes to surveying and understanding the overall landscape, marketers are the experts. No matter how you divide things up, there will be overlap, but, as with the vision system and other brain functions, more overlap leads to more flexibility and agility.

There is no one right way to integrate the approaches that I've outlined here. Nor are these methods necessarily the exact ones that you'll want to implement. But you will need to supplement your Agile practice with strategy practices. Furthermore, there is no right way to define the interfaces between your innovation methods and your Agile methods, but such interfaces must exist.

Smart companies are increasingly emphasizing the importance of linking these approaches. The blended culture that results will allow marketing to transition from a world of high-risk annual releases and Big-Bang marketing campaigns to one in which services are released frequently and at a steady cadence. In the future, no release would be able to fall so flat that it couldn't be rolled back with relative ease. At the same time, marketers will be able to tell just as many compelling stories about what's being released today as they will be able to tell about where things are headed. In fact, they'll be in a better position to establish better ways of selling, amplifying customer satisfaction, and tapping into latent demand from inside the product or service itself.

13

Beyond Agile: Marketing's Role in the Customer Experience

We've discussed product management's role as the steward of product strategy and innovation. Now let's turn to the marketer's role as the steward of the customer experience. According to a Gartner survey, by 2016, 89 percent of companies expect to compete mostly on the basis of customer experience, versus 36 percent four years ago.[1] I believe that the best way to start is to examine the customer experience your company creates across touchpoints, map that experience, and make it visible to the rest of the company. This exercise will reveal the gaps and the disconnects in a hard-hitting way.

Managing the customer experience across touchpoints can have a profound effect on your business. There is a $1 + 1 = 3$ effect that takes place when you align experience across touchpoints, such that the whole becomes greater than the sum of its parts. This is based on Gestalt psychology, the central principle of which is that the mind forms a global whole with self-organizing tendencies.[2] This idea was championed by the artist Joseph Albers, who explored chromatic interactions with flat, colored squares arranged concentrically on canvas. In Figure 3.4 (an example I drew in the style of Albers) there are only four squares, but their positioning and interaction creates additional shapes and content. There is a sense of depth that creates the impression that one is looking down a tunnel.

FIGURE 3.4 Example In The Style of Joseph Albers

Edward Tufte, a former professor of political science, statistics, and computer science at Yale University and an expert on visualizing data, articulates it best:

[The] visual activation of negative areas of white space ... illustrates the endlessly contextual and interactive nature of visual elements. This idea is captured in a fundamental principle of information design: $1 + 1 = 3$ or more. In the simplest case, when we draw two black lines, a third visual activity results, a bright white path between the lines.[3] [See Figure 3.5.]

FIGURE 3.5 $1 + 1 = 3$

Another example is the FedEx logo (see Figure 3.6), which creates an arrow in the negative space between the "e" and the "x." This is a clever and memorable visual cue that reflects FedEx's service, which is moving things forward.

These examples show how the $1 + 1 = 3$ effect works visually and how it might be used to advance a goal with visual meaning. But how does the theory work to support nongraphical experiences?

arrow in negative space

FIGURE 3.6   FedEx Logo With Arrow Outlined

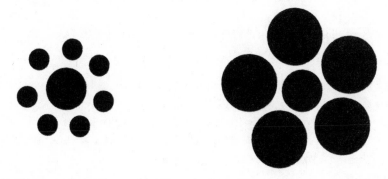

FIGURE 3.7   Gestalt Visual Effect Example

Let's consider how the theory might be applied in a restaurant context. Of the two images in Figure 3.7, which of the two center dots is larger?

As you've probably guessed, they are the same size, even though they appear different. Dan Ariely, the behavioral economist, presents a tangible interpretation of this visual slight in his book *Predictably Irrational*. In one study, Ariely placed the same quantity of food on two plates, one large and one small. He then gave 50 percent of his research participants the large plate and the other 50 percent the small plate. After eating from their respective plates, the subjects were asked how full they felt. Those who had been given the smaller plates rated themselves more satiated than those with the larger plates, although the two groups were given the same amount of food. The insight for the restaurant is that it could use smaller plates to reduce its cost of goods sold while still leaving its customers feeling equally satiated. Extrapolating this idea further, we realize that the customer experience can be manipulated through the context in which it is presented.

The Context of Customer Experience

Like the core service itself, the experience you design at each touchpoint benefits from iteration. There are a few sources of input that can be used to support iteration:

- **Feedback:** Feedback at the touchpoint (or following a series of touch-points) can be gathered using a range of methods, from observation to surveys.
- **Ideation:** Ideas can emerge internally, through crowdsourcing or some other practice.
- **Psychology insights:** Research into human behavior (as in the plate example above) can expose opportunities.

Avoid relying on a single source of input. Sometimes consumers will tell you exactly what they want, but they don't always know what they want until they see it, particularly if it is a brand-new concept. Remember what Henry Ford purportedly said: "If I had asked people what they wanted, they would have said faster horses." This is why testing and validation are so important.

When it comes to understanding human psychology and how to leverage it to support business goals, marketers have particular expertise. This is especially true if they have a formal marketing degree or psychology degree.

Dan Ariely presents another good example: an advertisement on the web-site of *The Economist* magazine offering three subscription choices:

1. A web-only subscription for $59
2. A print-only subscription for $125
3. A web and print subscription for $125

Any rational person who wanted a print subscription would choose option 3. Sure enough, when Ariely tested the three-choice offer, he found that 16 percent of the subjects chose option 1, 84 percent chose option 3 and no one chose option 2.

He then ran the experiment again, this time without offering option 2. The results were dramatically different: 68 percent of the subjects chose option 1 and only 32 percent chose the option for the web and print subscription. As Ariely explains, "option 2 in the first example was useless in the sense that no one wanted it, but it wasn't useless in the sense that it influenced the buyer's choice."

This option points to a psychological tendency that causes people to focus on comparisons between similar rather than dissimilar items. So, in the first experiment, potential subscribers are more likely to compare options 2 and 3 than they are to compare either of those with option 1. Thus, *The Economist* influenced where buyers focused their attention. (It's safe to assume that *The Economist* makes more revenue from its higher priced subscriptions.)

This example reflects the fact that people have limited cognitive resources, so they may not take the time to compare all available options. But be careful how you apply this insight; on the flip side, you don't want to present too many choices, because doing so can overwhelm the buyer and prevent any decision!

People don't actually know their preferences all that well; that's why we are so susceptible to context-related influences, such as option 2 in the first subscription experiment or the size of the plate in the previous example.

Even where there's an opportunity to leverage a psychological predisposition, testing and iteration will be critical to validate and optimize the effort. It would have been fascinating if Ariely had added more variations to his test to determine where pricing thresholds exist for the subscribers in question. Doing so could have made a huge impact on new customer acquisition and revenue generation, and possibly on customer satisfaction, as well.

Simplicity and Consistency First

The experiences we have with products and services across touchpoints are also influenced by these behavioral phenomena. Creating a consistent experience across touchpoints produces an overarching experience that, as we'll see, is greater than the sum of its parts. For this reason, marketers can deliver significant value simply by aligning experience across touchpoints and improving consistency. And there are ample opportunities to do this. Consider that, according to Accenture, 78 percent of customers have a fragmented experience as they pass through different channels—from web to retail location to 800 number.[4] On top of that, 77 percent of consumers report no relationship with a brand beyond the transaction.[5] Just think about the untapped brand opportunity this represents.

Aligning experiences across touchpoints is often easier said than done. The primary reason that touchpoints are disconnected is because they are managed by different silos within an organization. To align these silos, marketers must build bridges between them, working collaboratively and establishing common standards. For marketers, these standards are generally codified in the style guides and communication guides, although they are adopted more readily when they are positioned as knowledge resources. Of course, it helps when these resources are as lightweight and Agile as possible, that is, when they're principle-based rather than-rules-based.

Simplicity is the key, as principle 10 from the Agile Marketing Manifesto states (simplicity is essential). Simplicity is what staves off any clutter that fragments experience and obfuscates the marketer's message. It also makes aligning experiences across many touchpoints and channels more manageable, in turn allowing marketers to innovate more quickly. The path to simplicity can start just by trimming the number of assets you manage. A survey by DemandGen Report found that "75 percent of vendors give potential customers too much information to sort through" and "62 percent of customers state that much of the material is useless."[6] Imagine how much more effective companies could be if they channeled those resources otherwise—namely, into beefing up cross-touchpoint, cross-channel consistency.

Experience Strategy

Companies make these efforts because they recognize that experience isn't just about how the customer interacts with a product or service; it's about the customer's experience of a brand across touchpoints. Now, consider this: If a customer has a great experience at one touchpoint but a poor experience (or even just an inconsistent one) at another, is the net result the average of the two? Answer: not at all.

Research has shown that our satisfaction with a service is based almost entirely on the best or worst experience ("peak" experiences) we've had with the service and the most recent experience we've had with the service. The peak-end rule developed by the Nobel Prize-winning behavioral economist Daniel Kahneman illuminates much about customers' perceptions of their experiences with products and services that supports the need for consistency across touchpoints.

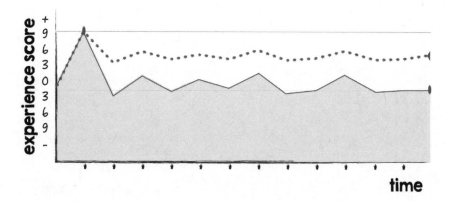

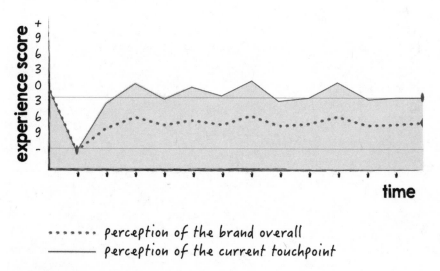

.... perception of the brand overall
———— perception of the current touchpoint

FIGURE 3.8 Peak End Rule Example 1

The experience map shown in Figure 3.8 depicts two scenarios: one in which the peak experience is pleasant and one in which it is unpleasant.

Though the average experience (represented by the total shaded area) is the same for all but two periods, the perceived experience is much greater in the top example. Even if you were to adjust the baseline of the bottom graph upward to accommodate for the shaded area lost in the unpleasant peak, the top graph would still come out way ahead.

Consider a second example that compares two positive peak experiences (see Figure 3.9).

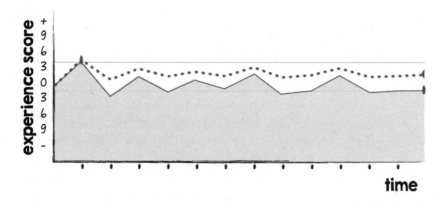

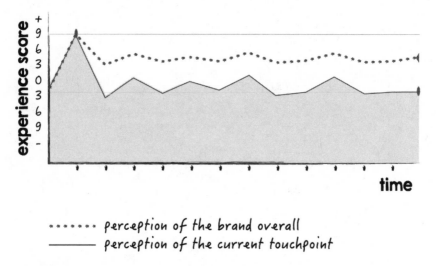

· · · · · · · perception of the brand overall
————— perception of the current touchpoint

FIGURE 3.9 Peak End Rule Example 2

Here, two positive peaks are contrasted. All points are the same except for the peak, which is higher for the bottom chart. Simply increasing the value of this one experience has a significant and lasting effect on the overall experience.

So what does this mean for managing experience across touchpoints? Based on this research, you can offer an average, or even slightly below average, experience so long as you offer your customers one truly great experience. If however, you allow even one unpleasant peak experience to take place across your touchpoints, it'll cost you dearly.

This brings us back to the importance of aligning and creating consistency across touchpoints. Integrating experience across touchpoints doesn't only promote consistency. It's an effective means of ensuring that you don't create an unpleasant peak for customers. It's also an excellent means of identifying the touchpoints that represent opportunities where you can really shine by creating a pleasant peak experience.

From Theory to Practice

The ability to measure customer experience is a prerequisite to implementing much of what I've laid out thus far in this chapter. Companies need a reliable way to measure the experience at each touchpoint, or across a series of touchpoints that users might engage with as they make their way through the buyer's journey or a customer support issue.

One of the most effective methods I know of is Bain's Net Promoter Score, which stands out for its simplicity. A company's Net Promoter Score is calculated from customer responses to a single question: "How likely is it that you would recommend [our brand] to a friend or colleague?" Respondents rate the company on a 0 to 10 scale; responses are grouped in the following categories:

- Promoters (a score of 9 to 10) are loyal enthusiasts who will keep buying and who refer others, thus fueling growth.
- Passives (score: 7 to 8) are satisfied but unenthusiastic customers who are receptive to competitive offerings.
- Detractors (score: 0 to 6) are unhappy customers who can damage your brand and impede growth through negative word-of-mouth.

Subtracting the percentage of detractors from the percentage of promoters yields the Net Promoter Score, which can range from a low of −100 (if every customer is a detractor) to a high of 100 (if every customer is a promoter). The Net Promoter score is optimized to measure customer experience in the short and long terms and reflects the peak-end rule.

With this research method in mind, what's the best way to improve the experience across touchpoints? As Bain's Bradley and Hatherall point out:

> Executives may be tempted to focus first on the episodes most likely to become highly distinctive, but the experiences of loyalty leaders suggest another approach. First, create a base level of consistent performance across the customer experience—by prioritizing and upgrading the episodes with the worst performance, or those that affect the highest number of high-value customers—then create points of differentiation.[7]

I'd expand on this advice to suggest a three-step process:

1. Eliminate negative peak experiences first, because these lead to long-term brand damage that is hard to recover from.
2. Simplify experience and ensure consistency, because this will inherently improve your baseline while helping identify the areas where you're most likely to be able to deliver a positive peak experience.
3. Develop positive peak experiences that will deliver a long-term benefit and distinguish your product or service.

Agile plays only a supporting role in this area of marketing practice. Looking across touchpoints requires a strategic perspective that emerges from mapping the customer lifecycle across touchpoints, as well as from conducting longer term research, which the marketing organization is equipped to do. Interpreting the data is an exercise—like the strategy exercises presented earlier—that requires collaboration across organizations. It also requires having data from the range of marketing systems that constitute the modern marketing platform.

The Chief Customer Officer: C-Suite Peer or Marketing Deputy?

In an increasingly social and transparent marketplace, controlling access to information is no longer a competitive advantage.

(continued)

(continued)

Although most companies aren't yet ready to do so, they will increasingly compete on the basis of the customer experience—a big benefit to customers. Integrated marketing services and the data they produce has become the foundation for improving the customer experience. Actually delivering a better experience, however, takes culture change—and leadership.

To that end, many companies are appointing chief customer officers (CCOs), although they are not defining the role very well. Moreover, it's unlikely that this role will follow the path of the chief product officer (CPO). Recall that with the rise of business technology, the product management leadership function often transitioned to the product development organization, in most cases, reporting directly to the CTO. Many younger companies in fact have realized that the product management lead needs to be elevated to the executive management level, and their CPOs now report directly to the CEO.

Most CCOs, despite their title, report directly to the CMO. They are not given the resources to effectively drive customer experience initiatives, nor are they empowered to direct their colleagues to drive such initiatives. Marketers control the lion's share of the customer-experience-related budget; that budget is distributed across marketing functions and is not directly managed by a CCO.

The CCO role will certainly evolve over time, but in my view, customer experience is something that needs to be led on an organizational level by the marketing function. Of all the initiatives that marketers oversee, customer experience is unique in the degree of collaboration it requires to deliver results. The CMO is effectively the true CCO, and more of a steward than an owner of the customer experience.

Modern Marketing and the Customer Experience

14 From Deeper Customer Relationship to Richer Customer Experience

To modernize the marketing function, companies must tap into a whole array of customer feedback gathered at multiple levels: direct user feedback, feedback from research, strategic feedback, and feedback that comes in the form of data flowing into your integrated marketing platform. Companies that are aligned internally to capture, analyze, and respond to all of these forms of customer feedback gain access to powerful marketing opportunities that arise out of a richer relationship with the customer.

Thus far we've looked at how feedback drives innovation and the facilitating role that marketing plays in this process. I presented marketing as the steward of the overall customer experience, but marketing is just as much the steward of the product's (or service's) community. After all, marketing is also the steward of the brand, and the modern marketer recognizes that the brand is no longer owned by the company. Scott Cook, co-founder of Intuit, said it best: "A brand is no longer what we tell the consumer it is—it is what consumers tell each other it is." Today, we are extending that concept beyond the brand to the entire product or service. And leading companies are beginning to grasp the notion that their communities of customers are not only their lifeblood but also, in effect, their innovation engine, marketing platform, and ultimately, their competitive advantage.

Increasingly, and especially in rapidly evolving industries, customers are not just buying what you're selling today. Like the Tesla customers I spoke of in Chapter 1, they are also buying a vision—a vision of where you're headed and of what your brand stands for. Undertaking an Agile transformation is vital for marketers, because it empowers them to take part in the product strategy and help shape the company's own vision.

That vision can be substantiated by a track record of delivering great experiences, by demonstrating your understanding of market trends, and with compelling narratives about how you're going to realize the vision. Smart buyers are looking for signs that you're agile (even if they don't call it that) because the ability to respond to the market quickly is the hall-mark of a successful, competitive company. Buyers learn more about how agile you are when they engage with your customers, rather than when they engage directly with your company or service. The community behind your product or service is generally your most powerful marketing engine.

A by-product of iterating *with* the customer is that the customer develops a sense of ownership of the product or service. In reality, it's far more than just a "sense" of ownership because the customers' input is what drives design and development. If there is a disconnect in this relationship, the customer will choose to "own" a different product or service. The goodwill associated with this sense of ownership can be transformed into value in two primary ways: one, through further engagement on the innovation front, and two, by leveraging the customer community as a marketing platform.

Your community of customers represents opportunities to expand your ability to upsell existing customers as well as to acquire new ones. Some of the most exciting and powerful opportunities can actually be built into your products and services. And the richer relationship you cultivate with customers will allow you to take advantage of these opportunities in an appropriate and effective manner.

In the following chapters, I'll share examples of how companies bake marketing into their products and services and how this can profoundly change their approach to advertising and promotion. We'll then examine the role that the community plays at practically every turn of the buyer's journey. Finally, we'll consider a new breed of company: one that embraces its community, and in doing so, has essentially pared its business down to the process of creating and managing marketplaces. Not all companies can do this, but all companies can learn important lessons from those that do.

15 Growth Hacking

The term *growth hacking* is shorthand for innovative marketing approaches that are best known for establishing and optimizing acquisition tactics—often with social functionality within the product or service—as an alternative to traditional paid media. Growth hackers are typically technical marketers who specialize in optimizing experiences such as landing pages and e-mail campaigns through activities such as A/B testing, which compares how two versions of an experience perform relative to each other. Growth hackers also scrutinize the product or service for opportunities to bake in marketing calls-to-action and other experiences that can drive awareness virally and fuel new customer acquisition. Sean Ellis, founder and CEO of Qualaroo, a website survey technology company, coined the term in 2010 to describe a set of marketing tactics used at start-ups whose mind-set was "growth first, budgets second."[1]

At an Agile Marketing Meetup in San Francisco, Ellis presented a case study on how he's applied growth hacking to his work as a marketer.[2] His approach is based on his extensive experience running growth teams at Log-MeIn, DropBox, EventBrite, and Lookout. There is a lot to know about growth hacking, but Ellis focused on a practice known as "high-tempo testing" that ties into some of the Agile practices that we've covered. This practice sets a target for the number of tests that get run in a specific period or sprint.

Ellis recounts how increasing the number of tests run each week correlated to a significant increase in the membership growth of his community site, Growthhackers.com (a great place, incidentally, to connect with growth marketers and Agile marketers). As soon as he required the team to increase the number of tests they ran each week, the trajectory of membership growth skyrocketed. Ellis pointed to similar results obtained by Satya Patel, the former vice president of product at Twitter, who drove a massive increase in membership growth when he asked the Twitter team to move from roughly one test every other week to 10 tests per week.

This small process change led to small changes in the service, which led to a huge change in the company's membership growth rate. Along the way, it forced Ellis's team to get skilled at running tests quickly. At the same time, it forced the team to break down tests into the most basic components possible: More tests meant less complicated tests. This concept comes straight out of Agile; Ellis's approach to growth hacking is really an Agile method—a variation of Scrum.

In the parlance of growth hacking, the Scrum Master is called a Growth Master. The backlog is a list of tests, instead of initiatives or features. Test ideas can be added to the backlog by anyone at the company, so they are crowdsourced internally. Further, tests are prioritized using a framework similar to the one presented in Chapter 12. Ellis's growth hacking method stipulates two types of tests:

1. **Tests to discover (pings):** These tests are designed to explore new channels or opportunities. Ellis used the example of the game Battleship, where players test coordinates on a grid to see if there is a battleship present at a specific location. If they get a hit, they focus additional fire in the same area; otherwise, they test elsewhere.
2. **Tests to optimize (A/B tests):** These tests aim to improve the effectiveness of content, experiences, or interactions by exposing subjects to slightly different variations. This type of test is also known as A/B testing or multivariate testing.

Apart from the framework Ellis uses at Growthhackers.com, there is another framework that growth hackers commonly use (see Figure 4.1).

This framework requires a baseline of activity to substantiate any test, so there are some circumstances in which running one is premature. This requirement actually highlights an issue for many Agile teams: relying too

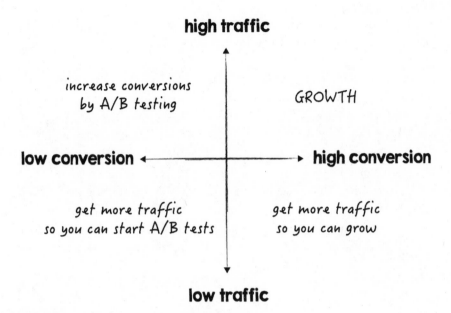

FIGURE 4.1 Growth Framework

heavily on feedback from a small set of users or research participants. Such feedback is not always representative of the feedback that would emerge from the overall market. So when it's not possible to run statistically significant tests, teams can pivot in the wrong direction. Nevertheless, statistical significance is not always possible to achieve in a timely manner, which is why it's so important to have a holistic innovation practice that can balance feedback from multiple sources—direct user feedback and strategic insights as well as tests.

Ellis noted that although running more tests led to an increased rate of growth, it is important to analyze how. It's not because each test adds incremental value; in fact, most tests fail to add value. It's because among many tests there will be a handful that make a huge difference. This is one example of the Lean concept of Kaizen discussed in Chapter 7: "small improvements that make a big impact." (Later in this chapter I'll share another example from my work at Involver.) First, I want to suggest a potential addition to the above framework that can promote balance and a regular cadence of success in the context of testing.

Testing is essentially an investment, and a sustainable and systematic approach to investment requires diversification in order to mitigate risk.

So in addition to prioritizing tests with the framework presented in Chapter 12, it's a good idea to evaluate the selection of tests you plan to run to ensure some diversity with respect to risk. Each test you run must have a hypothesis, and your confidence—with regard to this hypothesis being correct—will vary. Following this, it's worth including tests for which you have high confidence (lower risk) alongside tests for which you have low confidence (higher risk). Going back to Dan Ariely's example about *The Economist,* testing specific price points for the two initial options would have been relatively low risk. A successful test here would have revealed pricing thresholds that affect buying behavior. Whereas testing two pricing options against three pricing options would have been riskier (unless you were already aware of the underlying psychology), because it does not follow well-known patterns for optimizing pricing by adjusting price points to establish thresholds.

Growth Teams and Modernization

Growth hacking could conceivably be driven by product management or marketing. Like UX teams, growth teams have relevance in both contexts; in addition, they effectively link these functions. Unlike UX teams, however, growth teams are less prevalent, so it's rare to find an established growth team in both places. Instead, most companies struggle to determine where the growth team should sit—though, today, most eventually end up in product management. Some are actually stand-alone.

Wherever the growth team sits, it can be problematic because the initiatives that emerge from the growth team must be balanced with the other feedback sources we've talked about. These initiatives effectively add complexity to the reconciliation process outlined in Chapter 11. If companies don't balance feedback sources effectively, then conflicts can arise between the growth team, product management, and marketing. My view is that growth teams, like UX teams, should include representatives from both the marketing and product management sides to ensure close coordination between these groups. To be successful the ideas for initiatives that are germinated in this group must be integrated into the process that incorporates the full range of feedback sources used.

This level of coordination requires that company leaders buy into the promise of marketing modernization. Today this is still rare. Leaders often disassociate traditional marketing from more modern approaches, such as growth hacking. In many cases, they consider the latter approaches to be part of product management, not marketing. Hiten Shah, another growth marketer and co-founder and president of Kissmetrics (a web analytics company), put a finer point on this. In speaking about a CEO and marketer whom he admires, he said, "Ben Chestnut runs MailChimp [an e-mail marketing platform] and he basically hates marketing … but everything they do is marketing … they [just] think of it differently." Tesla's Elon Musk has also said that he hates marketing. These attitudes demonstrate the divide that persists in the marketing world between the traditional way of marketing and a more modern way.

Of course, when Chestnut says that he hates marketing, he's not thinking of Agile marketing; he's thinking of traditional marketing. The problem is that inspirational product leaders like Chestnut and Musk are more apt to talk about their dissatisfaction with the traditional approach than they are to acknowledge that there is, in fact, a new approach, and one that is working well for them. In practice, these leaders are brilliant marketers who have achieved their marketing success by applying Agile. Sadly, many such product leaders fail to champion Agile in a marketing context.

We can only hope that this will change as marketers increasingly adopt Agile practices and are able to show, through their results, how different modern marketing is from the traditional (and reactive) forms that product leaders often point to. Connecting marketing with Agile and Lean practices is likely the best way to facilitate a new mind-set because these leaders are, in fact, converts to the new approaches. This shift might also be fueled by the adoption of growth hacking beyond the start-up world, which we are starting to see. Indeed, growth hacking is not just for start-ups; it can be applied long after a company's initial growth phase. In fact, growth hacking is useful in a broad range of applications: improving customer retention, referral, revenue, resurrection—even acquisition and activation.

There are many more contemporary marketing practices that fall broadly under the rubric of growth hacking. They complement each other and can be combined in a number of ways to support your business. And all are compatible with an Agile approach.

Baked-In Marketing

Earlier, we established that adopting an Agile approach is an effective way for marketers to influence—and collaborate on—product and service strategy. Now, marketers can identify opportunities to leverage that influence to address marketing goals from within the core product or service.

Today, only a handful of services have a complete marketing solution built into them. There are many companies, however, that rely on baked-in marketing as a primary marketing strategy to drive marketing objectives such as awareness, adoption, and extension. Probably the most familiar example of baked-in marketing is the freemium concept: a pricing strategy that offers a product or service to customers for free but that also presents them with the opportunity to pay for more functionality. But marketing can be baked in to practically any service, especially if you broaden the concept of freemium.

Both of the social technology start-ups that I worked at leveraged a freemium model to drive awareness and demand. At Involver, we offered the most basic version of our applications for free. These applications garnered tremendous adoption because they were free, effective, and easy to use. By the end of 2012, our platform powered more than a million Facebook-enabled applications. Many of our apps contained Involver branding to which our freemium customers and their customers were exposed. The branding was minimal and appropriate but became a primary source of demand generation (it referred potential customers to our website). We also had calls-to-action within the administrative interface of our application for those who were actively using the freemium application at our lowest price point.

For example, the call-to-action would drive users to our free webinars. At these events, users could hear from Involver customers and learn about social strategy from our internal experts. But there were other marketing hooks in the administrative interface that didn't feel like marketing at all. Rather, they felt native to the application. For example, in one configuration screen we showed a setting that was partially grayed out, signaling that it was not active for some reason. When the user explored these settings (by mousing over them), they were presented with information about what those settings did, and they were informed that the underlying features were part of a paid offering. So, the call-to-action here asked users: Would they like to upgrade or try the feature for a limited time?

Meanwhile, in the background, we had an opportunity to track each user's behavior within the configuration area of the application and to scrutinize cues as to where they might be in the buyer's journey. We used an Eloqua (now Oracle Marketing Cloud) implementation that allowed us to score users based on their behaviors. We also relied on Eloqua's marketing automation platform, which supports nurture campaigns that are tailored to a wide range of demographic and behavioral signals (together, these signals constitute the prospects' and customers' digital body language). For example, we had a series of tips-and-tricks documents for our retail industry customers that could be delivered to just those users who explored the grayed-out features in our retail-oriented freemium apps.

As you'd expect, all of the information regarding whether these users read the tips-and-tricks e-mails could also be tracked inside the user record and synched with the CRM record that our sales team interacted with. The idea was if a prospect reached out to our sales team directly, a salesperson would be able to look up that user and see exactly what he had done and what content he'd received. Our goal was to educate and qualify users as much as possible before a salesperson engaged with them so that the salesperson would have insight into the customer's specific needs and interests. In that way, we could make the best use of our sales team's time.

Extending the Freemium Concept

In the freemium model, the opportunity to pay typically means providing deeper access to an application or service for a fee (as in the Involver example). But it can also be interpreted more broadly—that the freemium offering is outside of the core product or service. This concept is similar to that of a loss leader in which a company willingly sells something at a loss in order to create market opportunities. With the freemium model, companies accept a complete loss and chalk it up as a marketing expense.

Consider the Oracle Marketing Cloud (OMC) Topliners community, a resource for any marketer interested in learning about and discussing marketing automation and content marketing. Some 80 percent of the community members are not OMC customers. Topliners is such a rich resource for the marketing community that it's very much part of the service that OMC offers. In other words, this community is their freemium offering. As you'd expect, Topliners strategically presents freemium users with opportunities to raise their hands to get information about becoming paid customers. But why not just have a freemium version of the OMC core service? In this case, the marketing automation offering is highly complex, and there was no easy way to make a small portion of the service available as a freemium offering.

Gamification

One approach for accelerating your social sharing, testimonials, and social advocacy is known as gamification. Gamification is the use of game mechanics and game-design methods to influence behavior. Gamification taps into people's natural desire to express themselves, socialize, learn, and compete. It is most commonly used to stimulate these intrinsic desires, but it can include extrinsic rewards as well (such as payments).

Apart from fueling community engagement, gamification can also spur specific actions or behaviors. Consider how LinkedIn encourages members to complete their profiles. It presents the user with a measure of profile completeness ("profile strength").

People naturally want their profiles to be complete, so they follow the prescribed steps. This includes not only filling out their profile, but also connecting with other users or even inviting other users to join the service. That's a simple example of a product feature that drives adoption while extending the reach of the product.

The OMC Topliners' community employs gamification in a more sophisticated manner: It engages users and guides them down the path to becoming advocates. Users can earn points for sharing articles, best practices, feedback, or even submitting ideas for conference sessions at OMC's annual event, Modern Marketing Experience. And it can extend well beyond digital interactions. For example, Oracle's gamification platform supports check-in missions that reward customers for checking into different areas and booths located throughout the event. And (as you might have guessed by now), a gamification program lends itself to an Agile approach in that companies can start small with basic implementations and add breadth and complexity with each iteration.

Thinking about content, community experiences, events, and other programs in this context changes the way companies approach such programs. It forces them to think in terms of the value exchange that occurs during the buyer's journey. Establishing a fair value exchange here sets the company up for success later on, when it positions the value exchange associated with the purchase.

How much value you offer up front and how much you demand from the customer will depend on your product or service. If you're the only game in town, you'll have a lot of bargaining power, but in highly competitive markets, you'll obviously have less. Even in markets without much competition, having a generous value exchange can dramatically accelerate your acquisition of market share (although giving away too much can hinder conversion later on). Regardless of your competitive situation, you must discover how reliably your company can deliver that value. You want to be sure that *prospective* customers feel you have earned the right to present them with opportunities to become *paying* customers.

The freemium components of your marketing programs are limited to the value that you provide to customers on an ongoing basis, whether in the form of content, experiences, or services that benefit the customer. Your corporate marketing site is not part of your freemium offering, but an open community (like Topliners) that hosts a repository of free education content might be. Free trials and demos provide some value in the form of education, but should not be counted because they do not provide ongoing value.

Here are some examples that extend the freemium concept:

- **Google Trends:** gives away free insights into search behavior as a means of promoting Google's advertising platform.
- **LinkedIn Pulse:** provides users access to not only a free profile, but also to a publishing platform and a content feed as a means of promoting the company's paid services.
- **Nike Apps:** offers a range of free mobile applications that support the company's clothing business.
- **Bike Shop Air** (a program at many bike shops): offers free air stations for filling bike tires as a way to drive in-store traffic and purchases.

The freemium model can be configured in many ways. You may recall my talking about my experience working at an architecture firm in Boston (in Chapter 4). One of the ways that we drove awareness for the firm was by establishing an art gallery in the front lobby. The firm had done a unique renovation of the space that showed off its expertise, and the art gallery generated considerable traffic. The gallery was, in effect, our freemium offering to the community.

What you incorporate into your freemium offering will depend on your business. The freemium offering is an area in which you can be very creative, but it will take some amount of experimentation to land on just the right value exchange.

Frictionless Advocacy

At Involver, we not only baked selling opportunities into the configuration interface, we also embedded opportunities for our customers (including freemium customers) to promote us. Social sharing was the foundation of our approach. Facebook was still a relatively new channel for marketers at the time, and we ran an experiment that gave users who engaged in the configuration of our applications the ability to "like" our apps. Overnight that simple call-to-action increased the growth rate of our fan base fourfold. And more likes, of course, meant more Facebook users were being exposed to our company; in other words, we were extending our reach. Even better, potential customers were being introduced to our brand by their friends—a powerful form of endorsement. Because this took place early in Facebook's use of its EdgeRank algorithm (when posts by brands were visible to more users) the reach of these likes was far greater than it would be today, but you get the point. The marketing "ask" was embedded natively within the application experience.

Companies should always be looking for opportunities to ask customers for feedback from within the product, as well as fostering the kinds of engagement that lead to advocacy. At Involver, we hosted a Social Media Manager of the Year award program to identify potential advocates and to solicit great customer success stories. We promoted the program on our blog and in other channels, but embedding it in the interface might have been a much more effective way to reach our most active customers.

Businesses in almost every industry are moving toward a world driven by online advocacy. The examples here are mostly from within the software and technology world, but there are many nonsoftware examples. Moreover, many opportunities to embed marketing into the product exist at the intersection of the online and offline worlds. Consider New Belgium's Snapshot beer. This beer is named to inspire consumers to take photos of situations related to their enjoyment of the beer so they'll be inclined to share them online via Instagram. The company then uses these photos on its product packaging, in in-store displays, on its company website, and in advertising (technically, it's less like baked-in marketing and more like brewed-in marketing).

Advocacy needs to happen on multiple levels. Many companies give customers discounts in exchange for serving as reference customers. Others solicit customer stories by giving their customers the opportunity to develop their own personal brand by speaking at industry events and conferences. Some companies host hackathons and challenges for their communities. There are many more ways to create frictionless advocacy, from hashtags on Twitter to video comments on YouTube, to application experiences. The point is that modern marketers are building all kinds of exciting new ways for customers to advocate on their behalf, often without customers even thinking of it as advocacy.

Converged Media

Converged media presents a unique opportunity to take consumer goodwill, which is associated with social sharing (otherwise known as *earned media*) and give it even more reach. Converged media mixes two or more types of media channels: paid, owned, and earned (see Figure 4.2).

Paid media is simply advertisements that are purchased from a source that has aggregated an audience you want to reach, for example, a publisher. Earned media, as I mentioned earlier, is information about your company shared by your community without their being directly compensated. Owned media is any content you distribute via properties that you own or manage, such as your website or social property. When these types of media are converged, new opportunities arise for your brand.

What exactly do we mean by *converged*? The Altimeter Group (recently acquired by Prophet, a research and advisory firm), defines it well:

Converged media ... is characterized by a consistent storyline, look, and feel. All channels work in concert, enabling brands to reach customers exactly where, how, and when they want, regardless of channel, medium, or device, online or offline. With the customer journey between devices, channels, and media becoming increasingly complex, and new forms of technology only making it more so, this strategy of paid/owned/earned confluence makes marketers impervious to the disruption caused by emerging technologies.[3]

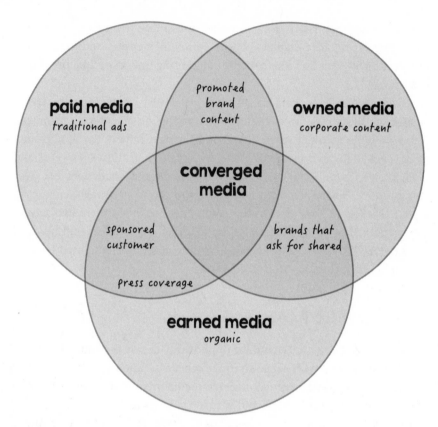

FIGURE 4.2 Paid, Owned, Earned Media Venn Diagram

Let's take a specific example. On Facebook, it's possible to amplify a consumer's testimonial about a product or service beyond the user's own network. In Figure 4.2, this is represented as sponsored customer content.

Converged media is powerful because it often promotes content that is more trusted than traditional media. Now, consider how rare a commodity trust is these days: according to the Edelman Trust Barometer,[4] half of the countries surveyed had trust levels in business below 50 percent. And according to BazaarVoice, "over half of Americans (51%) trust user-generated content (UGC) more than other information on a company website (16%) or news articles about the company (14%) when looking for information about a brand, product, or service."[5] Clearly, converged media is much more effective than traditional paid media because people trust their peers more than companies, analysts, and pretty much anyone else.

Native Advertising: Paid Media That Feels Like Earned Media

Some companies have pioneered forms of paid media that are almost indistinguishable from earned media. Consider Warby Parker, the online eyewear company. With only a handful of locations, this retailer has managed to disrupt traditional retail vendors with a service that delivers eyeglass frames to your door to try at your leisure and without commitment. That's *its* free service.

Warby Parker advertises through podcasts, but the company doesn't overtly indicate that it is the podcast sponsor. Instead it asks the host to take the audience on the journey to buy a new pair of glasses. The host first asks the audience to vote on which frames he should try by taking input via social media. In the podcast's next episode, the host shares a story about the experience of receiving the frames, proclaiming how nice the packaging was. Between episodes, he posts on his social accounts pictures of himself wearing each set of frames, and asks his listeners to vote on which pair they like best. In so doing, the host shares a credible endorsement of the experience while generating paid media that is indistinguishable from earned media.

With this podcast, Warby Parker has created much more than an advertisement; it has developed scalable content that can be used across a range of marketing programs, from automated communications to events. In addition, the assets are more credible, and thus more effective, because podcast listeners generally trust the podcast host (why else would they listen?). Warby Parker can always amplify its paid/earned media with direct paid media from its own channels. Finally, what makes the approach even more powerful is that Warby Parker has inspired hundreds of people to create "try on" posts and videos of their own to solicit feedback on their frames from their friends. Each and every one of these responses gives the company an opportunity to amplify a consumer message with converged media.

Podcasts are, of course, just one approach to native advertising. You can expect native advertising to become more prominent in the coming years—that is, if you can identify it for what it is!

16

Lessons from the Collaborative Economy

In Chapter 12, I discussed how connecting external and internal communities can support ideation and drive innovation. Now let's look at companies that have externalized much of the work that internal communities—that is, their employees—do.

Traditional businesses across a wide swath of industries are being disrupted by a new breed of company that leverages communities as the foundation of its business. You've probably guessed I'm talking about companies such as Airbnb, Uber, Etsy, Instacart, Upwork, Lending Club, Indiegogo, Instructables, and many others. These companies are creating new business models in which one community—providers (formerly employees)—serves another community—customers. Most people refer to this phenomenon as the rise of the *sharing economy*. Others call it the *collaborative economy*, a term I prefer because of its broader implications. (Sharing economy is confusing, because it suggests free exchange or bartering, when, in fact, this economy, for the most part, involves exchanging money to make a profit.)

Jeremiah Owyang of Crowd Companies offers what might be the best definition of the collaborative economy: "an economic movement where common (i.e., everyday) technologies enable people to get what they want from each other." Look up Owyang's infographic, the Collaborative Economy Honeycomb, online to see just how far and wide the movement has spread. (Incidentally, this infographic, which has been updated numerous times, is a wonderful example of how to effectively iterate on a piece of marketing content to improve its value over time.)[1] As of this writing, Owyang's graphic represents more than 150 companies across 12 industries, from health care and transportation to financial services and food services.

While the terms collaborative economy and sharing economy are relatively new, the type of economy they refer to predates the likes of eBay, Craigslist, and open-source software. In fact, the concept of improving the utilization rate of assets and resources such as tools, shelter, seeds, and money is as old as history itself. Indeed, businesses have always had to determine which elements of the value chain they should own and which ones are best subcontracted (or outsourced) out.

Today's collaborative economy, however, is very different in two respects. For one thing, it has reached an inflection point: The business models that power it have hit critical mass in the marketplace (as evidenced by their disruption of established business in so many industries). In addition, the degree to which processes are externalized is more far-reaching than ever. In the digital era, technology allows the outsourcing of many more processes (sometimes even invisibly to the end customer). This capability means that these new business models can take root in far more industries and sectors. Taking the idea to the extreme leads us to ask: "Just how far can you pare down a business while still delivering innovation and an outstanding customer experience?" We'll take that on later, after we explore how these changes are affecting more traditional businesses.

Collaborative Companies Reset Expectations for Traditional Business

Many traditional businesses (and that includes many established tech companies) are still transitioning from business models predicated on the company's ability to direct demand and consumer preference. Their organizational structures and processes haven't kept pace with the empowerment customers have gained through social media and other contemporary communication channels. Today, most businesses are still figuring out how to effectively engage their customers in a more transparent and open manner.

Collaborative economy companies, on the other hand, have gone beyond empowering the customer and enabling the customer's voice to shape the product. They are tapping into the emerging community of providers—working people outside of the traditional labor force. Unlike employees in traditional businesses, who submit to the ways of the company culture, the external workforce that powers the collaborative economy comes to the table with that higher level of expectation that consumers now possess. In other words, they feel entitled to share their opinions and views openly with the intention of influencing the business.

Even companies that don't formally enlist providers in lieu of employees will feel the impact of this new force. Increasingly, employees will be demanding the same kinds of opportunities to provide feedback and input. After all, employees are also consumers; if they aren't already doing business with disruptive companies, they will very likely be doing so soon. In some cases, they may be supplementing their salary by working as providers to those companies' businesses (as many Uber drivers are doing). These relationships, moreover, are capturing much attention—in the media, in the online world, and in the general culture. And as this new business model takes hold, the pressure on companies to listen to employees, and not just their customers, will only increase. This is yet another reason that connecting internal employees with external providers and customers alike is becoming so important.

Companies that rely on an external workforce to produce their product or service must now actively address feedback from two external groups: the customer (or end consumer) and the worker (or provider; what Jeremiah Owyang refers to as "empowered people"). This feedback from both sides holds tremendous sway in shaping products and services. (See the sidebar, "Me and Airbnb.") The power of Agile, as a critical tool for iterating, becomes even greater when applied to two sources of community feedback.

Me and Airbnb: This Author's Experience as a Provider in the Collaborative Economy

I was already well familiar with the consumer side of the collaborative economy as a user of Craigslist, eBay, Uber, Etsy, and the Munchery. But to write credibly about the provider side, it seemed

(continued)

(*continued*)

only right that I had some firsthand experience. To that end, my wife and I bounced around the idea of becoming Airbnb hosts. Our home already has a guest room with its own entrance, which meant we could rent out accommodations without having to provide access to our entire house. Undeterred by the flurry of e-mails from my mother—who, upon learning about our experiment, informed us that our toddler was about to be kidnapped—we went ahead and signed up.

Getting up and running was a cinch. Within days, we had our first guest—and our first positive review. We also received feedback: Our customer suggested we provide tea and mugs in the room. So with the income from that first guest we bought an electric kettle and a selection of teas (we already had matching mugs). That got me thinking about what else I could do to make the experience special. My wife made fun of me for doing so, but I made a mix of relaxing music, just like the kind luxury hotels have playing when guests arrive.

After two months, we had hosted 17 different guests from six countries. Each month we earned enough income to cover about a third of our mortgage (although I'm planning to use the money for something a little more fun). I continued to make improvements along the way, such as offering a hidden key in case our guests lock themselves out of their room. So far, we've had only one negative experience: an untidy guest.

In addition, I've been collecting feedback for Airbnb. Every time a guest stays with us they have an opportunity to rate us (as their hosts) and provide feedback on Airbnb's site, and we have the opportunity to rate them as guests. Moreover, we can provide private feedback to Airbnb about the guest. This ultimately allows Airbnb and its hosts to be more selective about which guests to host.

I'm also collecting my feedback to give to Airbnb about its core service—and I expect the company to listen. I've participated in Airbnb research that, one hopes, will lead to service enhancements. And I also submitted feedback to the company

(*continued*)

(*continued*)

about the fact that my wife and I cannot easily manage our home listing together. To do so she must use my login on her computer and mobile phone. I tweeted the following message:

"@Airbnb: Are you working on making it possible for family members to manage a listing without sharing the same login?"

Within five minutes I got the following response:

"@rsmartly: Not currently, but that's a great idea! We'll make sure to pass it along to the right team."

What became clear to me through this experience is the fact that collaborative-economy companies like Airbnb provide a particularly rich feedback environment for all parties. They've established feedback channels within specific product areas as well as channels for general feedback via the web, e-mail, and social. Consumers expect to be heard, providers expect to be heard, and even Airbnb expects to be heard. The company, for example, offers pricing tips to hosts based on historical data and statistical analysis.

I predict that all this feedback will have an impact on consumer and employee expectations. Imagine, for a moment, a hotel concierge who rents out a room in her home to make some extra money. Like me, this host would expect to be able to provide feedback to Airbnb in an open and transparent manner. When this host goes to work as a regular employee, she won't leave these expectations at home. Rather, this experience will change her baseline expectations about her employer's willingness to accept feedback.

Experiencing provider feedback, either as a user of a collaborative economy service or as a provider of one, won't cause a cultural shift overnight. But as employees of traditional businesses are increasingly exposed to the experience, their companies will not be able to ignore their heightened awareness. And that will become an increasingly important factor for companies to consider as they fight to recruit and retain the best talent.

How Disruptive Will the Collaborative Economy Be?

The collaborative economy stretches across multiple industries. But how deep is its impact? Airbnb offers a clue. By 2015, its seventh year of existence, the hospitality company's market capitalization had hit more than $25 billion. Compare that with its older, mainstream competitors, such as Starwood Hotels and Resorts (market capitalization in 2015: $14 billion), InterContinental Hotels ($10 billion), and Hyatt (just over $8 billion). Airbnb is also grabbing overall market share; a recent Boston University study demonstrated that for "every 1% increase in Airbnb bookings there is a .05% decrease in hotel revenue."[2]

This same pattern is playing out across other industries. In fact, looking across the entire landscape, PricewaterhouseCoopers predicts that the collaborative economy will grow from $15 billion to $335 billion over the next 10 years.[3] Such explosive growth in an otherwise slow-growing global economy represents a real threat to traditional business. So how are traditional businesses responding to the prospect of being disrupted, if not out of business then out of their market position? The responses cover the gamut, from attempting to obstruct collaborative-based businesses altogether to proactively embracing the collaborative business model to some extent.

- **Legislation:** Collaborative economy businesses often operate at the edge of existing legal frameworks that favor the traditional-economy businesses for which they were designed. Traditional companies can therefore exercise their influence to hinder the growth of disruptive businesses. Several cities and hotels have challenged Airbnb's business with lawsuits. (Workers' unions are also raising opposition, as the collaborative economy models threaten their influence.)
- **Acquisition:** Traditional businesses can acquire the start-ups that could potentially disrupt their businesses. Unfortunately, this is often literally disruptive to the acquired company, because the traditional business does not understand it well enough to manage the integration process effectively. The best acquisitions tend to require a lengthy transition period during which the traditional business and the acquired business evolve toward each other. Of course, this extended honeymoon can slow innovation, leaving the newly combined company open to more competitive threats from new start-ups.

- **Partnership:** Some traditional companies will seek opportunities to partner with disruptive companies to facilitate their transition to a new business model or to supplement their existing model. Toy manufacturer Hasbro chose to partner with Shapeways rather than bring legal action against the company for allowing consumers to augment and make 3-D models of its characters. Most likely nothing would have stopped superfans from 3-D printing their characters, but by reframing the threat as an opportunity, Hasbro added value in the form of legal access and convenience.

- **Emulation:** Finally, some companies might adopt a new business model within their overall corporate structure and actively emulate their disruptive competitors. For example, Starwood Hotels might create a high-end version of Airbnb that is more upscale and trustworthy. In addition to expanding its inventory, Starwood could utilize its existing service force for cleaning and maintenance. It could even use its current loyalty programs to market the new offering.

Agile and the Collaborative Economy: Three Business Models

It's no surprise that the rise of the collaborative economy coincides with the rise of Agile Marketing. The two reflect a new mind-set, one in which community feedback is integral to product development. The rise of the collaborative economy actually amplifies the need for—and usefulness of—Agile. That's because the collaborative economy, like Agile, is dependent on community feedback, from the community of users as well as the provider community. Agile is designed to accommodate a high level of engagement among participants to constantly adapt and improve processes and products.

There are three related business models associated with the collaborative economy. To an unprecedented degree, they have all outsourced elements of the business to the crowd, which enables them to provide a greater return on investment to their customers. In some cases, this means reducing the cost of a service (as with Airbnb); in others, it means providing a better service at a comparable cost (like Uber). Companies that embrace these models dedicate more resources to sensing and responding to feedback from their two basic communities: customers/users and the empowered people, providers.

Model #1: Empowers the Community to Define the Product or Service

By establishing platforms to leverage input and insights from their community, companies based on this model give the community ownership in their products and incentivize members to champion their use. We've already looked at crowdsourcing as a way of driving innovation. A specific example of this is My Starbucks Idea, which we discussed in Chapter 12.

Model #2: Turns the Product into a Service

Instead of selling their products to customers in a one-time transaction, companies can produce fewer products overall while maximizing their value by selling their use. A good contemporary example is cloud computing. Perhaps the most famous example of turning a product into a service or *servicization* is Rolls-Royce's "Power-by-the-Hour" offer. In the 1980s, Rolls-Royce started selling the use of its airplane engines on a cost-per-hour basis. Rolled up in this service is the entire cost of supporting, servicing, and maintaining the engine. This alternative business model changes the incentives for Rolls-Royce: Instead of revenues being dependent on the sale, repair, or maintenance of engines, they are now directly connected to engine air-time. An added benefit to customers (and the company's brand): From a design perspective, this approach shifts the focus away from cost effectiveness and back to quality and reliability. And consider this hypothetical example: A few years from now, once self-driving cars hit the market, you might not buy a Tesla, but you might opt to use Tesla-as-a-service, just as you'd use Uber today. Or, perhaps Tesla and Uber will partner to develop this business jointly. (And why not? They have some big shareholders in common.)

Model #3: Creates a Marketplace for Service Providers

Instead of providing the service itself, the company operates a marketplace where service providers can transact with customers directly. Perhaps the most famous example of an entire business based on this model is eBay; others include uShip, 99designs, and Lending Club. And traditional businesses can adopt this model to augment their established operations. That's what Swisscom has done in collaboration with Mila. (See the sidebar, "Swisscom Taps into Crowd-Based Tech Support.")

CASE STUDY: SWISSCOM TAPS INTO CROWD-BASED TECH SUPPORT

Swisscom, Switzerland's largest telecommunications company, has long differentiated its service by offering an exceptional customer experience. Swisscom serves as a trusted advisor to its customers for telephony and related digital services. In late 2013, the company went one step further by launching a peer-to-peer tech support marketplace called Swisscom Friends. The marketplace is one of the first of its kind, in which residential customers can find local support (vetted by customers and Swisscom) to help solve their tech problems—everything from setting up a wireless router to configuring a phone.

Swisscom Friends is the latest offering in a portfolio of support options for the company's customers, who can already take advantage of such free services as an online support community and retail-location-based technicians. But Swisscom Friends is cheaper than making an appointment for a Swisscom field technician to make a site visit.

To launch the new service Swisscom partnered with Mila, a Switzerland-based general service platform that helps large companies build their own their own local service marketplaces and tap into the collaborative economy. Like TaskRabbit, a U.S.-based competitor, it lets users rate and review service providers and consumers.

For Swisscom Friends, Mila established a new marketplace just for Swisscom that included approved providers. "With the collaborative economy, we've found that some customers actually trust the crowd more than the company that provides the service," says Ursula Oesterle, vice president of innovation at Swisscom. "Indeed, this initiative has had a very positive impact on overall customer satisfaction while reducing the average time to service and resolution."

The program is not without financial benefit, of course; Swisscom earns a small fee from each community transaction (the average transaction is between $80 and $100) and has trimmed the support

(continued)

(*continued*)

costs of its free channels (those retail-location-based technicians). More important, says Oesterle, Swisscom's initiative had the effect of strengthening its relationship with the crowd. In its first 12 months, Swisscom Friends won 1,500 new friends, and it continues to add about 100 new friends a month, according to Mila.

Because anyone can tap into the Swisscom Friends network, Swisscom Friends is actually extending the company's relationships beyond the customer base. So a non-Swisscom customer who needs help setting up e-mail on his iPhone can get help from a neighbor who uses the service. As with customer transactions, Swisscom charges a modest transaction fee. But the real value to the company comes from the goodwill generated with potential customers. "Swisscom Friends was never about revenue generation," says Oesterle. "It was about customer experience and satisfaction first, and [only] then about reducing the cost of providing support."

Swisscom isn't the only winner here. Beyond the transaction fee it earns, it gains validation from working with Switzerland's premium telephony provider. And when Swisscom Friends' users need help outside of telephony needs, they turn to Mila for support.

Companies like Airbnb effectively combine the first and third models. They empower the community to define the product; they act as steward of the marketplace; and they also provide regulation. There is a stunning variety of properties on Airbnb's site—from traditional homes to tree houses and Airstream trailers—because hosts define what the guest experience will be at their properties. But there are also ample ground rules and constraints to protect both sides.

Servicization's Impact on Incentives

The most dominant theme underlying the three collaborative business models is the shift from an ownership mentality to a user mentality. Certainly, this shift can't be applied to everything we exchange (I'd rather not share my toothbrush), but it will cause us to think about every exchange in a new light. This is especially true at a time of growing global awareness of limited resources, concerns about waste, and the importance of recycling and reusing. So, perhaps I'll subscribe to a toothbrush service that sends me new brushes at the right frequency and then turns my old brushes into, say, fleece jackets when I'm done with them.

Of the three business models, servicization has the greatest potential to transform business. The reason is because it has the greatest potential to impact both the economic incentives to the business and the customer experience. The benefits of servicization are very specific to the value of the product itself, that is, for the company, the cost of production and for the customer, the cost of paying for the service versus buying the product outright. In general, servicization is seen as a way to reduce a capital expense and free up resources—and in the process, gain agility. Servicization allows businesses to focus resources on value creation rather than on lower value operations that require hard assets. It can be used effectively to align business incentives. Rolls-Royce, for example, made the move to ensure engine reliability; this served the customer's needs better than the previous model, in which the company made more money when its engines broke down.

Businesses that embrace these new models must think carefully about how the new incentives will impact their relationship with customers. Just as Dan Ariely's restaurant experiment (which placed the same amount of food on a large plate as on a small plate) changed the diner's perception of being full, your choice of business model can have a significant impact on customer perception and satisfaction in sometimes subtle, if not unnoticeable, ways.

Will customers do the detailed math necessary to calculate and compare the total cost of ownership versus the cost of a service over time? The answer may create an opportunity for companies, for example, to take advantage of the fact that consumers acclimate to recurring fees (those that renew a service automatically or with minimal effort). In other cases, such as automobile leases, consumers may be willing to pay a premium for the ability to cancel a subscription at any time. But just how much of a premium? If companies don't navigate these new market spaces adeptly, they risk a profound backlash from the crowd. A 2015 headline from *Business Insider* declared, "Uber Drivers Speak Out: We're Making a Lot Less Money than Uber Is Telling People." Similar episodes are likely to play out as companies and the crowd get used to these new and disruptive business models.

Now that we've put the impact of the collaborative economy in context, let's return to our earlier question, "Just how far can a business pare itself down while still delivering innovation and an outstanding customer experience?" At the most basic level, a company must be able to do these five things:

1. Identify a market need
2. Provide a basic solution to address that need
3. Communicate about the solution and accept feedback in return
4. Apply feedback to iteration to improve the product/market fit
5. Monetize the solution to sustain further improvement

In other words, it's hypothetically possible to pare things down to the Agile process—the process that's at the heart of value creation for collaborative economy companies.

The relationship between companies and the crowd is evolving quickly. While this presents an extraordinary new opportunity for marketers, it also represents a significant risk to companies if they don't get it right. That's where Agile has a major role to play. Smart marketers will leverage Agile to validate direction, iterate on what's working, mitigate risk, and pivot as necessary.

So what role does business play when it creates a platform where people can get what they want from each other? It provides a framework for exchange. A company's ability to adapt that framework to the evolving needs of its customers and its providers will ultimately become the measure of its success.

Conclusion: The Steward of Customer Experience

Throughout this book, I've presented stories about companies that are working hard to modernize and about companies that are dramatically disrupting established business models. They share a common denominator: the view that their communities (both internal and external) are a resource—in fact, *the* critical resource—that must be leveraged to sustain competitive advantage. We've explored the role that Agile can play in facilitating community engagement to support both innovation and marketing. Agile not only harnesses input from the community, but it also provides a better approach to developing the integrated marketing platform that marketers will need to better understand and engage with the community.

As a discipline shared by the innovation and marketing sides, Agile is also strengthening C-suite relationships where it gains a foothold, even where traditional strategy practices remain in place. And that's a good thing: Every member of the C-suite has a vested interest in an integrated marketing platform that supports his or her goals. The marketer's ability to deliver this platform as a service to his or her colleagues (MaaS) is a long-term, but nonetheless worthwhile, goal that will uniquely position marketers to be the stewards of customer experience—and thus turn Peter Drucker's vision into reality.

How should companies be thinking about customer experience in the larger sense?

Oracle is one of those big companies that is fighting hard to modernize. Due to our size and complexity we are also one of the most challenging environments in which to apply the concepts of Agile marketing. In the next several pages, I share our experiences with modernizing marketing. While we have a long way to go, I hope our efforts and progress thus far will inspire you to apply some of the concepts we've explored throughout this book at your company.

The Customer Life Cycle

To understand the customer experience, it must be seen in a larger context: that of the complete customer life cycle. Recall the experience map from Chapter 13 that represented customer experience in a linear manner to illustrate its component parts. But the customer experience is actually cyclical. At Oracle we represent this life cycle as an infinite loop (see Figure 4.2).

The loop consists of a *buy* side (a.k.a., the buyer's journey), where we focus on marketing and selling; and an *own* side that represents the support and services that help the customer succeed with our products and go on to adopt our latest service enhancements. This double loop depicts a more holistic view of the customer experience, encouraging Oracle marketers to compare customer experiences that would otherwise be managed in silos.

In fact, even at opposite ends of this double loop some experiences intersect. For example, individuals who are researching a product or service increasingly want to experience what it's like to own or use it before they actually commit to buying. They often do this by joining the community of existing customers where they congregate online. Following this, they visit a touchpoint on the own side of the life cycle while they are still technically on the buy side.

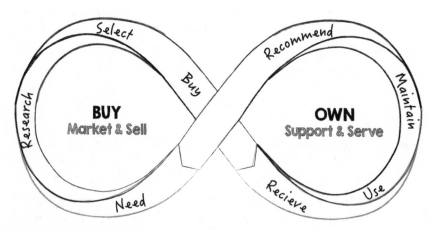

FIGURE 4.3 Customer Lifecycle

Which brings us back to a theme I first presented in the book's introduction:

> *With the rise of social media, marketers entered an era of heightened exposure in which any kind of product or brand failure has the potential to echo virally and at lightning speed through the marketplace. This vulnerability has intensified the pressure on companies to treat customers better and to share information with them in a more transparent manner. And the information sharing has evolved to include the active solicitation of feedback to incorporate at increasingly earlier stages of the product cycle.*

This heightened exposure works both ways. If companies deliver an outstanding customer experience throughout the entire life cycle, they stand to benefit. But in order to benefit, they must make the effort of evaluating the customer experience at every touchpoint in the customer life cycle. And they must compare the customer experiences at opposite ends of the journey, because that's exactly what customers are doing when they engage with the company's community at the start of their buyer's journey: They investigate how the company interacts with and serves its existing customers.

So what qualifies marketers to lead the effort of ensuring an excellent customer experience throughout the customer life cycle? Essentially, three capabilities:

1. Out of every team in the organization, marketers have the most experience engaging with the community.
2. Marketers are the ones building the platform to aggregate all the data that is tracked along the entire span of the customer life cycle that will inform the analysis.
3. Marketers are already managing all brand-related interactions.

The Community Influences the Entire Customer Life Cycle

At Oracle, we found that the customer life cycle—particularly the buyer's journey portion of it—has been changing. In the past, procurement at client companies was carried out in a top-down fashion. Today, different individuals are participating at each phase of the customer life cycle. Procurement is now a mixed bag—partly top-down and partly bottom-up. In the enterprise technology world, the tech practitioners at client companies—the customers who actually use the products—are gaining greater influence in corporate tech procurement decisions.

This trend plays out in ways big and small. On a small scale, practitioners bring the technology they use in their personal lives into the workplace. Perhaps the most pronounced area where this is happening is with social media. Employees have acclimated to the personal use of social media tools that have been designed and optimized around individuals' mobile behaviors. This practice has reset the expectations that people bring into the workplace as users, and overall, as customers.

On a large scale, senior buyers (financial buyers and sponsors) are increasingly relying on detailed analysis done by practitioners on their teams to make purchasing decisions. At Oracle, we see this playing out at nearly every turn of the buyer's journey. When practitioners are asked to evaluate a product or service, one of the first steps is usually to search for articles and reviews of Oracle technologies (if they haven't first gotten a recommendation from a friend or colleague). We work hard to make sure that they find articles and reviews from Oracle advocates at the top of their search results. We do this by cultivating relationships with the members of our flagship advocacy program, the Oracle ACE program. Members of this program are highly influential technical experts who are outspoken about Oracle technologies. To get into the program, applicants must author technical papers or articles and develop other content that helps the community succeed with Oracle technologies.

Most important, Oracle does not tell ACEs what to write or how to write it. In some cases, ACEs' content undergoes a technical review, but otherwise they are free to express their opinions. And those opinions are not always flattering. But we are confident that, overall, the content will be positive, because our members have chosen to build their careers around our technology. We value the credibility they bring through their substantive evaluations as well as their experience with competitive products, which allows them to put our technology in context.

ACEs develop a lot of substantive content. But they are also active on social media because they want to build their own brands as consultants and to work for top companies. As you'd expect, we promote this earned media to extend its reach. So practitioners may initially come across ACE content on social media. A practitioner might watch one of our "Two-Minute Tech Tip" video interviews that feature ACEs. If they do, they'll be more likely to take the next step in the buyer's journey, which is to download trial software or sign up for a cloud trial. ACEs often provide the initial "social proof" that practitioners are looking for before taking the next step in the journey.

Engaging Practitioners before the Buy ━

Many marketers hold a misconception about trials, demos, and free samples of any kind: They believe that these offerings answer most of the buyer's questions. In reality, buyers typically have more questions during and after a trial than before, and these later-stage questions tend to be more specific. It's at this point that buyers turn to the user community for social proof. Buyers in this phase seek three things from the community:

1. Confirmation that a community already exists, because no one wants to be the only customer of your product or service.
2. Assurance that you are participating, listening, and contributing.
3. An indication that the community is satisfied with your products or services.

If practitioners find what they are looking for they'll be willing to advocate for the purchase and to reengage the financial buyer in the process. But note that the practitioner's involvement is not over yet. Once the financial buyer makes it through the procurement process, the practitioner generally reengages with the community—almost immediately.

Oracle has a number of communities. Virtually every customer relies on our peer-to-peer community—the Oracle Technology Network (OTN)—to some degree. Customers can receive training and certification from Oracle University, which has its own community. The MyOracle Support community is for users who are paying for support, and some of them will join the Oracle Partner Network (OPN). It is from these communities that we often identify the next generation of ACEs who will contribute the technical articles, testimonials, and demos that the next generation of buyers will find at the start of their journey.

This Oracle example illustrates where communities fit within the customer life cycle in the enterprise technology sector. But it's easy to pinpoint the elements that apply across industries. The specifics of the journey will be different: Some companies may lack an owned community or a community of technical experts like our ACEs, but there will nonetheless be a community of customers who will be engaging with each other. And as we've seen generally across industries, end users (that is, user buyers rather than financial buyers) are more engaged in the buyer's journey. Crowd engagement in consumer services came years before it did in enterprise services. Yelp.com, for example, started business reviews in 2004, whereas the first crowd-review sites for enterprise IT (such as ITCentral Station and G2 Crowd) were launched as recently as 2011.

At a time of rapid technological innovation, it's also interesting to see how the buyer's journey is being affected by younger generations. And I'm not just referring to young practitioners influencing senior management; I'm also talking about kids influencing their parents. Today, young people are able to make more informed buying decisions for themselves than their parents could, at least in certain areas, such as mobile telephony. It's not only because they are digital natives, either. It's also because younger generations—including millennials—come to the table with more pronounced expectations of transparency. They're more likely to influence—and be influenced by—the crowd conversation. And they're more likely to be guiding the purchasing decisions of their elders.

In my own life, I'm increasingly informing the purchasing decisions of my parents. This is especially the case with my father, who has Parkinson's disease. He struggles to keep up with technological innovation—with Internet technology, with banking services, and even with health care coverage. This is a complex and highly sensitive situation, and one that would be even more challenging to face alone. At some point, my brother and I will be the primary buyers, and we'll continue to rely on the crowd for guidance and help as we research the best services to support him.

So, the challenge of any business today is to map the customer life cycle and identify opportunities to better leverage your community. When you look across your touchpoints, is the customer experience consistent and positive? Do you know which parties in your organization play a role in the journey? To answer these questions properly, you need to analyze the data collected from across all of those touchpoints.

Data and Customer Experience Go Hand in Hand

The Oracle example illustrates the opportunity companies have to leverage the community at nearly every turn of the customer life cycle. It also underscores the importance of collecting data throughout the entire life cycle. This data is a crucial input for business intelligence systems, and it supports deeper consumer insights that would otherwise be hard to obtain. (Remember: Information gaps undermine insights, and you need a complete data set to identify and eliminate bad experiences.) For example, business intelligence tools can help identify correlations between community behavior and buying behavior. At Oracle, for instance, we discovered that 86 percent of corporate customers that have at least one user actively engaged in the OMC Topliners community renew their subscriptions. Moreover, companies without at least one engaged user renew at a significantly lower rate. So, active participation in our community is predictive of buying behavior—in this case, the likelihood of renewal.

Presumably, this is because those companies with actively engaged users are more likely to be successful with their product usage based on the support available within the community and the input of their peers. Community engagement data supports this theory. But participating in communities also leads to the formation of relationships that have emotional value for the customer. These relationships compel customers to support each other, to overcome obstacles together—even to compete with each other (for example, to see who gets the best results, or who wins "most voted on" product idea). These competitive behaviors can be amplified and measured through the use of gamification data and then correlated with financial data.

A modern marketing platform—one that is integrated—aggregates and manages these kinds of data sources in a consistent manner to facilitate their use in improving the customer experience throughout the life cycle. At Oracle, we established a new customer database to aggregate data and make it accessible to our business intelligence service. This, in turn, will enable my community team to get quicker answers to a broad range of business questions such as:

- What service-use behaviors are characteristic of potential advocates?
- Do different customer segments exhibit different buying behavior patterns?
- Which content resonates best with which audiences and at which particular points in the buyer's journey?
- Which product features do your most loyal customers use most?
- How does this compare to the features that your most profitable customers use most?
- Which product features do your most vocal advocates use most?

- Are there correlations between support-ticket creation and user training and certification?

The salient point here is that a modern marketing platform is a data platform that supports not only marketing but also every business unit of the company. It can be used not only to answer specific questions but also to explore the data in ways that unearth answers to questions you wouldn't have necessarily known to ask. Of course, it also allows each business unit to shorten the feedback loop and act in a more Agile fashion. Critically important for growth hacking, such a platform enables this activity in a scalable fashion and does not require one-off development projects to get the data needed to support individual business decisions. That's the core service and the payoff of the integrated marketing platform as a service.

So how did we go about establishing this service at Oracle?

Let me preface the answer by admitting that it's been a long journey, and we still have quite a ways to go. Also keep in mind that in the past three years, Oracle has acquired more marketing technology companies than any other company in the world. At the same time we've embarked on an ambitious modernization initiative to upgrade our own marketing platform using internally developed Oracle technologies (such as Oracle Database) alongside the new ones we've acquired.

To put this effort in perspective, when we started out, our platform was built on several technologies that were 10 to 15 years old. The platform serves 1,000-plus marketers and handles millions of leads, hundreds of millions of website visits, and billions of social interactions related to more than 4,000 products. Suffice it to say that we understood why all the major analyst firms were reporting that marketing data isn't integrated inside the enterprise. And, mind you, Oracle is at the larger and more complex end of the spectrum. The fact is that few marketing technologies are designed for our level of scale and complexity out of the box. And for the biggest companies, it's simply not possible to build a new platform, turn it on, and switch off the old one. Rather, companies must go through a transition period during which the old and new systems run in parallel as they migrate programs from one to the other. As a result, at Oracle, we needed to coordinate a rollout of new services with a migration of programs.

As a company that sells customer experience solutions, we must demonstrate the power of our technologies in order to credibly market them, even if that means designing these services for a scale beyond the needs of most of our customers. At the heart of our marketing modernization initiative was the understanding that investments in customer experience were a means of paying forward our ability to retain customers who were undertaking the same sort of transformation that we were embarking on. Of course, building a great customer experience is just as much about retaining customers as it is about acquiring new ones. (It's a well-established fact that retaining an existing customer is much less costly than acquiring a new one.) So, retention was a key success criterion for our initiative. This is also why we're working hard to incorporate data from our community platform into our customer experience database (CXD), which is the foundation of our modernization effort.

CXD is built on the Oracle database, and leverages Oracle-engineered systems to support real-time services. From the start, we adopted a robust architecture that would support a range of modernization objectives from improved search to robust mobile experiences, web personalization, and marketing automation. Today the CXD aggregates data from both legacy systems (such as our Siebel databases) and data from new systems such as our Oracle Marketing Cloud services (social, marketing automation, data, and so forth). As you'd expect, CXD is integrated with our Oracle Sales Cloud to give our sales force a more complete picture of customers' digital body language and pinpoint where they are in their customer journeys.

Bence Gazdag led the team that implemented the first iteration of our customer experience database. His group, which is part of marketing operations, had limited experience with Agile but committed to an Agile approach based on the complexity and unknown scope of this initiative. Besides connecting with Agile leaders in the product development organization, Gazdag invested in launching the new initiative with a teamwide Scrum certification course. While initially he got some pushback, the team quickly adopted aspects of Scrum. As with many teams that are new to Agile, Gazdag's people found Scrum to be too prescriptive at first, so they cherry-picked the practices they wanted to follow. Ongoing support at the executive level helped keep Gazdag's team focused on making Agile work and carried them through the first iterations to the point where they could see the value for themselves.

The team quickly discovered that there were valuable data sources that had previously been inaccessible due to the latency associated with legacy systems. When these systems were initially put in place, marketing automation platforms didn't even exist, so making data accessible in real-time was simply not a requirement.

As the team progressed from iteration to iteration, they integrated more data sources and started developing APIs that would make it possible for each service to pull enriched data back from CXD, where it was cleaned and validated. Then, when they integrated Oracle Social Relationship Management and third-party data sources with CXD, they were able to start unifying social identities with existing contacts in the database. This was the last dependency required to implement the most ambitious element of the CXD initiative to date, topic scoring.

Topic scoring is a concept developed by the marketing automation world. It is based on user behavior, both online and offline. The topic scoring model looks at customer behavior across all data sources—event attendance, social interactions, website visits, downloads, and so on—and assigns a score to each activity based on the degree to which it indicates interest in a topic. That score maps to a hierarchy of topics that are relevant to Oracle's business. For example, if a potential customer visits the Oracle Marketing Cloud Blog and reads a post about content management, she might be assigned points for the Content Marketing topic. If she then downloads a whitepaper on the same topic, she'll be assigned even more points on that topic. For Oracle to assign a score to a specific user, we obviously need to know who the user is based on a browser cookie or site registration. But we also collect topic scores based on anonymous data such as an IP address, which can give us insight at the company level.

An individual's topic score is an ever-evolving set of values that are affected by actions taken across touchpoints. We also aggregate individual topic scores at the company level. With this data, any connected service, such as a website or events registration service, can query the CXD when that user arrives and present the user with the most relevant information based on her leading topic scores at that moment. This is a very powerful service—and one that requires governance. Just as you would not have a salesperson call a customer at the very moment you observe that they've returned to your website, the services that leverage the CXD API must do so in an appropriate and strategic manner. We therefore manage access to the CXD API via our security and legal review board. For those teams that merit access, this is an ideal source of data to support web personalization. At Oracle, the scale of such data inputs are orders of magnitude greater than those most social scientists would typically have access to, which means that it's possible to obtain statistically relevant results very quickly. This, in turn, supports faster iteration. (See the sidebar, "Big Data, Digital Body Language, and Governance.")

Agile has served Oracle well in our marketing modernization effort. We are still far from fully leveraging the value contained within CXD, but in just two years we've upgraded our core platform and migrated the first set of programs. Building the platform is only half the effort, though. Getting each line of business educated about the new marketing service and getting it up and running with services that leverage the data in the CXD can take just as long. Our strategy has been to focus on key initiatives that will inspire others to innovate with us. To that end, we've established a new role focused on evangelizing the service internally and getting pilot projects off the ground. It's been an exciting journey to witness and to be part of.

CASE STUDY: BIG DATA, DIGITAL BODY LANGUAGE, AND GOVERNANCE

Big Data promises to unlock deeper insights into customer behaviors and preferences, which, in turn, support personalization across touchpoints. It also enables the best possible customer experience. The picture Big Data provides of the customer reveals his digital body language. While the data that reflects the customer's posture is of immense value, it can also be used in ways that undermine the business. In fact, companies must adopt a posture of their own that reflects their appropriate and safe use of data.

Case in point: Target's algorithm that identifies pregnant women and their approximate due dates based on their purchasing behavior.[1] Andrew Pole, the company's statistician, developed his prediction engine by analyzing the purchasing behavior of women who had birth registries with Target. He then analyzed the purchasing behavior of women who did not have registries to spot purchasing patterns that matched the first group. Those women with look-alike purchasing behaviors were presented with coupons for maternity products. In one instance, Target received

(continued)

(*continued*)

complaints from the father of a teenage girl; he was infuriated that such mailings were being sent to his daughter, whom he felt was too young for such products. The father later apologized to Target after discovering that his daughter was, in fact, pregnant. Interestingly, Target also discovered that women who felt targeted by the ads did not respond positively. As a result, the company adopted a more subtle approach that put the maternity coupons among other offers and content. This softened the company's approach and produced better results.

Target's experience shows how important it is that companies apply the insights available from Big Data in a sensible fashion—appropriately and respectfully. It also speaks to the inherent value and sensitivity associated with customer data. As companies aggregate and organize more and more data, marketers must take security more seriously. That includes working with the other business functions to establish clear and responsible governance policies about the use of customer data. In the past marketers avoided such concerns, just as they avoided dealing with the technology that enabled their digital experiences. That's no longer an option.

Embarking on the Marketing Modernization Journey

In Part 1 of this book, I described the uniquely challenging moment in which we as marketers find ourselves. I spoke of a chasm that divides us from extraordinary new possibilities. Figuratively, that chasm is the gap in the adoption curve for a wealth of new marketing technologies. But it also, more literally, represents an obstacle that must be overcome. That's the challenge of marketing modernization.

We marketers also find ourselves at a pivotal moment in another sense. We now face a test: We've worked hard to convince our peers that we're poised to lead and that we now have all the right stuff (technology and practices) to make it across the chasm. We have an opportunity to assume true leadership status within our organizations while also elevating the discipline of marketing. We could not have made this claim five years ago or arguably even a year ago. We've just reached the cusp now. It's no longer a question of whether, but of when—and of who among us will lead the charge. By reading this far, you have demonstrated that you're interested in being one of those leaders. You understand that succeeding will not only help you grow your company's business, but it will establish you as a modern marketing leader.

Marketing modernization is a journey. As with any Agile project, it's impossible to say up front how you'll get from your current state to a modernized state. What's more, modernization is more than just a plan, it's fundamentally about culture change and transformation. (This is the sense in which Peter Drucker said "culture eats strategy for breakfast.") This transformation goes beyond what I've covered in these pages; my goal has been to provide insight into how marketing practices are changing and what it takes to develop a modern marketing platform. Clearly, what's happening in the marketing area is representative of how Agile will impact other parts of the business.

Marketers are still in the early stages of this transformation. There is no one right way to achieve marketing modernization (or Agile transformation, for that matter). Best practices will emerge. For now, you cannot go wrong relying on the values and principles of the Agile Marketing Manifesto. And while you're at it, pay close attention to the efforts of smaller organizations, as these companies will continue to be the pioneers.

Building on the to-do list I shared at the end of Part 2, let me offer five general recommendations on how to foster marketing modernization in your organization:

1. Implement the principles associated with the Agile Marketing Manifesto.
2. Create discrete marketing services that add value to your customer experience database.
3. Integrate with other organizations in an Agile fashion (i.e., fostering an Agile transformation) to enrich your customer experience database.
4. Look for opportunistic ways to integrate marketing into your products or services.
5. Act as the steward of the overall customer experience.

I've also included some resources at the back of this book to get you started.

I hope this book has inspired you to think seriously about Agile, to start talking it up in your organization. Much more important, though, is that you *do* Agile. Thought leadership brought Agile into the marketer's world; but it's *do leadership* that is what's most needed now. So the sooner you embrace Agile, the sooner you'll obtain the feedback you need to iterate with. Although being an early adopter is not always easy, having first mover advantage is powerful.

You will not be alone in your journey. There is already a community of marketers who are passionate about Agile. Just as buyers seek a community to guide them in their journey, so too, you'll want to be part of a community of marketers who share your aspirations—and who are using Agile with success to achieve them. Connect with them, and support one another. Your community is bigger than just the community of marketers; it includes all Agile practitioners. That also includes your product leader. So connect with him or her (or them), too, because they will be your primary partners in your endeavor to build an Agile culture.

Onward. It's time to make Drucker's vision a reality.

Appendix 1:
Content Marketing:
An Agile Approach

Content marketing is a practice focused on communicating messages that influence buying behavior and other business goals. Unlike traditional advertising, content marketing tends to focus on establishing a relationship with a prospect or customer over time through the delivery of value-rich content. In this way, content marketing is fundamentally about nurturing a relationship to impact progression through the customer life cycle. It is a softer approach when it comes to selling and attempts to avoid messages that come across as sales pitches. Instead, it aims to educate and entertain potential customers as a means of establishing trust. For existing customers, it aims to support adoption, customer success, and promote loyalty.

Across the customer life cycle content marketing supports a broad range of business goals. Think about it: Almost every touchpoint that a customer interacts with involves some form of content, whether digital or traditional in format. Content marketing serves a range of specific business goals. It organizes and sequences different types of content to systematically drive prospects down the sales and marketing funnel (the buy-side of the customer life cycle in the diagram presented in the Conclusion), as well as down an advocacy funnel (the own-side).

One of the most common challenges that marketers face today is how to manage all of this content, which in recent years has been proliferating. As we noted in Chapter 13, many prospective customers are, in fact, overwhelmed by the amount of content that they are deluged with. One of the major reasons for this is the lack of a coherent and coordinated content marketing strategy. Throughout organizational silos, many different teams are creating similar content for the same prospect or customer. Companies need to build a framework that organizes—and sequences—their marketing content in accordance with the specific business goals each type serves. Such a framework can facilitate the development of a complete content portfolio to address the needs of your prospects and customers at every stage of the customer life cycle. It is also designed to:

- Improve the effectiveness of your content through iteration.
- Improve the customer experience by filling gaps in your content portfolio.
- Simplify your content portfolio by reducing the overall volume of content and channels through which it is disseminated.

For much of the latter half of this book, I explored the alignment of product management and marketing with an emphasis on embedding marketing into the product or service. Here, I focus on content that is primarily delivered outside of the core product or service, although these ideas can also help you manage the ancillary content associated with your product or service—everything from signage to product copy, training documents, and in-app notifications.

The content marketing framework is made up of a series of eight exercises:

1. List business goals
2. Define content themes
3. Define personas
4. Inventory channels
5. Define content types
6. Link content attributes
7. Fill content gaps
8. Consolidate channels and content

These exercises, which build on each other, are meant to be performed on a regular basis. Their output constitutes the core of your content marketing strategy.

Exercise 1: List Business Goals

Content serves a broad range of business goals; everything from repositioning a brand to educating prospects and from qualifying demand to driving

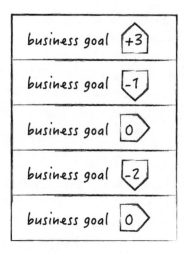

FIGURE 6.1 Prioritized Goal List

adopting. A great way to launch your content strategy process is to create a list of every high-level business goal that your content team will be asked to address.

This list should be posted in an easily accessible place where business stakeholders—including product management and sales—can review and provide feedback on an ongoing basis. Additionally, I recommend prioritizing this list so that stakeholders see a ranked representation that reflects what your team is working on at any given moment. This list should be revised on a quarterly basis. Adding a "+/– change" value that represents the most recent ranking change (how many positions did the goal move up/+ or down/–) to each goal can help communicate changes since the last update (see Figure 6.1).

Generally speaking, this list will also reflect your overall business strategy because your current goals should all connect back to that strategy—though it may be necessary to create such a list for each business unit if they have unique goals, objectives, and content needs.

Exercise 2: Define Content Themes

Your content themes serve as a consistent thread throughout all the content that you create. For instance, the Oracle Marketing Cloud (OMC) weaves the idea of marketing modernization through the content they create. In fact they've even developed a character named Modern Mark, who is the lead character is a video series that follows his modernization journey. As you'd expect, Modern Mark turns up at events and in other contexts to reinforce this theme in a consistent fashion.

Perhaps you have already articulated your content themes within an existing hierarchy of messaging. If so, you'll need to validate that they support your business goals and are consistent with customer feedback. This will ensure that your themes are current and consistent. As with business goals, the messaging hierarchy should be made accessible to all stakeholders and should be updated a least once a quarter. (Note that showing changes in this document is not as easy as it is with the business goals list because the content themes document can be lengthy and text-intensive.)

As with your business goals, your content themes should be agreed upon and defined by executive leadership and then communicated to each team developing content. Many companies assemble an editorial board that is managed by the marketing group but that also includes representatives from product management and other lines of business.

To facilitate the development of your messaging hierarchy, I suggest reviewing the following practices:

- Reconciling various feedback sources (described in Chapter 11)
- Developing your high-level strategy document (described in Chapter 12)

This will not only help reinforce your understanding of the messaging that is important to the company, but it will also help you understand which messaging resonates with prospects and customers. Online advertising can be an effective means of testing messaging with prospects and customers, although traditional market research approaches can work just as well for companies in less rapidly evolving industries.

Exercise 3: Define Personas

Personas have become increasingly popular with marketers, designers, and product managers, ever since Alan Cooper popularized them in his 1998 book, *The Inmates Are Running the Asylum*. Today, they are essential for

Agile marketing teams, and represent another front on which marketing and product management should actively collaborate.

Personas are fictitious characters, or archetypes, that represent prospects and customer types in a dossier format. They typically include psychographic, demographic, geographic, and behavioral information. Personas essentially enable marketers and designers to empathize more easily with potential prospects and customers because they seem like real people. Productive discussions emerge from questions about how one persona might react to a piece of content compared to another.

Personas are a resource that marketing should make available to all teams within the company. They should be revised over time, to expand them and give them more depth. Ideally, personas should be based on research; they should not be invented or even based on anecdotal experience with your users. Younger companies (like Involver, my former company) generally have relatively basic personas compared to what we use at Oracle. And that's completely appropriate; at Involver, we had a much smaller product set, were working in a newer business area, and thus had a smaller set of prospect and customer types. In addition, our typical sale was much less complex. See Figure 6.2 for a sample design for a basic persona.

In this example, the persona layout includes a proper name but also gives the persona a name that can function as a nickname. For example, at Involver we had personas with the names, "Head Honcho," "Social Guru," and "Rockstar Creative." Such monikers are good reminders of the persona's role when team members don't yet recognize the proper names.

The layout calls out key themes and the content types that are relevant for this persona, which links them to your content strategy. This example also captures information about what kind of buyer-type the persona is. In a B2B context this might include sponsor buyer, financial buyer, or user buyer. In a B2C context, it might include such descriptors as parent or sibling.

Next is a short, written description of the persona and a set of user dimensions that capture where the persona sits within a specified range. For example, in the B2B context, the range might represent how internal- or external-facing the persona's role is. In a B2C retail context, it might represent how fashion savvy the persona is. The dimensions you choose to include will, of course, vary by persona.

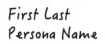

First Last
Persona Name

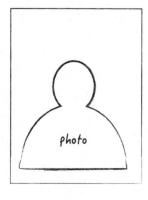

photo

title:
company:
company type:
location:
buyer type:
skills:
gender:
age:

Description
description of the persona, description of
the persona, description of the persona,
description of the persona, description of
the persona, description of the persona,
description of the persona.

Key Themes
theme
theme
theeme

Key Content Types
content type
content type
content type
content type
content type

User Dimentions

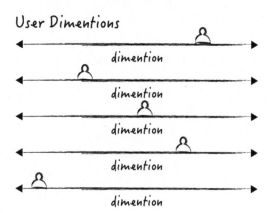

dimention

dimention

dimention

dimention

dimention

FIGURE 6.2 Lightweight Persona Example

The personas we use at Oracle expand on the basic example above to include:

- A detailed job description
- A list of top business concerns
- Key pain points
- Relevant opportunities
- Key business priorities

- Industry trends affecting the persona
- Organizational positioning

Personas are useful not only for inferring how users might respond to different features or experiences, but also for helping validate content, design concepts, and minimum viable products. They cannot replace testing with real prospects and customers, but they can help identify potential trouble spots before you invest in testing. In fact, I must emphasize that personas should not prevent you from testing and from engaging with real people to validate your content. They are not intended to represent a person; rather they are representative examples of a type of prospect or customer. Their real value stems from the discussions they foster during content development and from their ability to put content performance in perspective.

Exercise 4: Inventory Channels

One reason for the proliferation of content is the proliferation of new marketing channels. Social media evolves at such a breakneck pace that it's tempting to explore new channels on a monthly basis. Having an inventory of active channels not only helps manage this proliferation, but it also helps you experiment with new channels when it is appropriate to do so.

The best place to start is to inventory the channels that you already have in place today. If your company is like most businesses, you will find different channels have been set up and are managed by different people. So, create a table that includes each channel name along with the current manager. You'll want to group channels in a way that makes it easy to sort them; for example, set up a group for "social channels" (e.g., Twitter, Facebook) and then list each handle or identity as a subgroup under each channel. For the moment, don't worry about channels that you might want to use in the future (we'll get to those later).

The next step is to define the overall organic reach of each channel. On Facebook, for example, this would be the number of followers, and for a web property it would be your monthly unique visitors. (We'll use this metric again in Exercise 8.) Finally, if there is already a documented growth rate associated with the channel, capture it in your table. It's best to represent this as a positive or negative percentage.

Exercise 5: Define Content Types

The goal here is to list and define the content types that you distribute (or would like to distribute) through available channels. In my experience, teams sometimes struggle with this exercise because they confuse content types with channels or format. For example, a blog post is not a content type; it's a content format delivered via the blog channel (website). A weekly fashion tip is a content type that a fashion retailer might create as a post on its blog but which might also be reformatted as a tweet for a Twitter channel. (For clarification, refer to the section on content cupcakes in Chapter 10.)

The list you create will serve as the first column of a table that you'll build out with the following exercises. You can also capture a list of content types that you don't currently create today but that you'd like to consider creating. Internally crowdsourcing a backlog of content types is another great way to facilitate collaboration across teams.

If you need help getting the ideas flowing, inspire your people to think about how content types fit into the following grid. Here, "awareness" represents the top stages of the sales and marketing funnel and "purchase" represents the bottom stages. The emotional-to-rational scale can help suggest content for different personas that is appropriate for different channels (see Figure 6.3).

As you try to map your content into the above grid don't overlook user-generated content. For example, brands like North Face prompt users to share photos from their adventures (in North Face gear, of course) by awarding $100 gift cards for the best entries on a weekly basis. Curated selections are then used to adorn North Face collateral and product pages. Many companies have demonstrated that presenting user-generated content in this way helps such pages outperform their own studio photography. And in its converged media program, North Face can extend the reach of this earned media with paid support.

User-generated content plays an important role in content strategy. (Refer back to Chapter 15 where I discuss the role of user-generated content and how it functions in the context of converged media.) Although it may go beyond your current content strategy, you ought to think about the experiences that you offer to your community that will lead to user-generated content. They might be social application experiences, review sites, games, in-product opportunities, or other experiences.

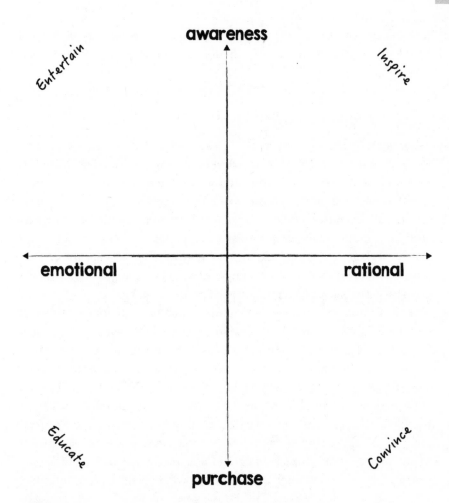

FIGURE 6.3 Content Development Framework

Exercise 6: Link Content Attributes

This exercise builds on the resources that you've created with the first five exercises by linking the attributes of your content. You can now create a table: Your list of content types serves as the first column, and you create additional columns for content type, content themes, relevant personas, and associated channels. Filling out this table effectively creates a sortable content grid that will allow you to find relevant content by channel, persona, or theme.

To expand this table further, we'll consider each content type through three lenses and add columns for frequency, formality, funnel stage, and content source.

Lens 1: Frequency and Formality

Frequency indicates how often you'll create—or update—the given content type. Formality indicates the general level of resource investment and polish that the content type requires. Frequency and formality tend to be inversely related; formal messages go out less often; informal messages, more often. The formal content generally offers more depth and breadth. For example, it's quite common to create informal social content at relatively high frequency (such as social posts that feature quotes and images that are relevant to your audience) that promote a more formal asset that gets updated on a quarterly basis (such as a white paper or product catalog).

Rank all your content by frequency and formality. A simple way to start is to create a five-point scale. Your most frequent content type, say a "quote of the day" that you publish on one of your Twitter channels, would get a ranking of 1, whereas content that you update every six months might get a 5. Now, take the same approach to defining the formality of each content type.

Once complete, you should quickly be able to get a sense of how balanced your content types are with respect to formality and frequency. As a general rule, you should end up with content pyramid, in which there is a greater overall volume of informal content and a lower overall volume of formal content. The degree to which this is the case will depend on your business.

Lens 2: Funnel Stage

Some content types are intended for—and perform best at—the top of the funnel; others are meant for the bottom. This positioning, if you will, is distinct from formality; it has to do with where the prospect is in the buyer's journey or where the customer is on the path to becoming an advocate.

Defining the stages within your sales and marketing funnel (or your advocacy funnel) is a prerequisite for this exercise. It also requires collaboration with sales and product management. The criteria defining an individual's funnel stage should be revisited every quarter to best manage the flow of prospects through the funnel. You'll likely discover bottlenecks that can be addressed with content changes or by adjusting the criteria to enter each stage. Such criteria changes can ensure that salespeople have an appropriate volume of leads, or that leads are sufficiently well qualified. Such changes will result from feedback from sales and prospects (refer to Chapter 3 for the discussion on ramping up marketing automation and coordinating with sales). They will also invariably impact your marketing automation programs.

Once you have determined the stages and the criteria an individual must meet to be at any given stage, you can then add a column to your table for the stage that each content type is intended for. Note that some content types will work for more than one stage; when that's the case, simply denote the stage where the content is intended to have the biggest impact.

When defining a stage for each content type, it's best to start with the source content rather than derivative content (sometimes referred to as *atomized* content) that results from slicing and dicing the source content. Again, the derivative content will generally be less formal and higher in frequency. Such content also tends to lend itself to social channels (such as Facebook) rather than owned channels (such as your own website).

Looking across your table, it's now possible to discern patterns in your content portfolio. For example, social channels tend to be useful for top-of-the-funnel stages, whereas owned channels tend to be more effective for bottom-of-the-funnel stages.

Lens 3: Derivative Content

Content drives prospects and customers down the funnel to conversion to becoming either a customer or an advocate. Content may be distributed in different formats to perform at different funnel stages. For example, action camera maker GoPro uses social posts that include videos on Facebook and Twitter to entice potential customers to learn more about the company and its products. These same videos also entice existing customers to post their own videos.

These short-form videos (or atomized content units) fit into a rich gallery experience on GoPro's website. There, GoPro has more flexibility and control to present longer form videos and sequences of videos to tell stories that engage users more deeply. (This example is similar to the one presented in Chapter 10 about slicing and dicing a book into derivative content cupcakes.) GoPro repurposes content in different formats to impact behavior at different stages of the funnel.

This derivative-content exercise is about linking source content types to derivative content types by notating the actual source of the content (or simply the fact that the content is source content) in the last column of your table. Typically, derivative content types are used at a higher funnel stage than the source content, but not always. You'll discover that while there may be dominant patterns of content consumption that drive users down your funnel, different types of people (personas) will make their way down the funnel via different content pathways. That's fine, and it's entirely appropriate. You couldn't possibly design content specifically for each consumption pattern. But as long as you have a complete content grid, your prospects and customers should be able to find the right content at the right time to meet their needs.

Derivative content is an area where marketing automation can make a huge impact. That's because it helps ensure that the right people get the right content via the right channel at the right time, based on data you've gathered about how they interact with the content. Remember, marketing automation is providing you constant feedback on the performance of your content, which can be addressed with each iteration of that content—and each iteration of the automated programs that serve content to prospects and customers.

Exercise 7: Fill Content Gaps

At this point you should have a fleshed-out content grid, along with a set of stand-alone documents that support it. This grid will allow you to analyze your content and identify gaps in your portfolio. You may discover that you do not have content types or assets for every persona or every stage of your funnel. Any gaps you identify should be added to your content-types backlog.

As you look for gaps, keep in mind that you may currently be using a particular content type (or individual asset, such as a product catalog) at multiple stages. This is common for companies that are still building out their portfolios. It also represents an opportunity to slice and dice source content in ways that reformat it and make it more effective at different stages. Note, however, that when you create derivative content, you must always tie it back to one of your business goals. And it must always add value; it is counterproductive to slice and dice content just because you can.

Consider, for example, a bicycle manufacturer that publishes an online guide for bike maintenance (featuring its bikes, of course). The company might initially refer traffic to this asset from a range of channels that serve audiences at different stages. This could be an opportunity to slice and dice that guide into discrete video demos that have embedded links to the full guide (such as YouTube cards that overlay clickable links on a video). These might work better on social channels or managed channels where the consumer can watch a video without leaving the mobile app. But should the company take the top 10 takeaways (or statistics about bike repair) from the larger guide as the basis for an infographic that serves this same stage? That will depend on whether the video approach meets the needs for all personas during the awareness stage. Perhaps there are only certain personas for whom an infographic is more compelling. If so, it might be worth exploring.

The final step in filling gaps involves comparing specific content assets. Thus far, we've talked about content types rather than the specific assets that you'll create. Say our bike manufacturer has a content type called "education guides." Within this category, the company might have two assets: one about bike maintenance and one about riding skills. These may be intended for different personas and for different stages in the funnel; many riders, especially those just learning bike-riding techniques, are likely not yet ready to learn about maintaining their bike. It's therefore important to break out the specific assets that fit under each content type in your table. There are two categories of assets that will emerge during this process:

1. Reference content that you periodically revise
2. Serial content that builds on themes

Reference content should be listed out in your content grid because you'll iterate it over time. Serialized content, however, should be listed as a content type because you won't want to list every single bike-riding tips-and-tricks post that you publish on your blog. Simply insert "serialized" to indicate the nature of the content type you are producing. Be aware that it's smart to review serialized content on a quarterly basis to seek opportunities to update and republish. This effectively entails iterating on the content, which is far more efficient than creating new content each time.

Finally, gaps are not just areas in which you are lacking assets. Gaps are also areas where the content that you have is underperforming. So it's useful to color-code the content in your grid to highlight the content types that are performing well. Although there are industry benchmarks for content performance, the performance of your content is ultimately unique to your business. Thus, it's important to track performance according to content type.

Exercise 8: Consolidate Channels and Content

Apart from identifying gaps through Exercise 7, you may also discover that you have multiple content types intended for the same personas with the same purpose at the same stage. This represents a clear opportunity for consolidation. As a general rule, having fewer high-quality assets is better than having a larger number of lower quality assets—particularly when it comes to your reference, or source, content. For serialized content, meeting a minimum publishing frequency may be required to garner an audience for some channels such as blogs. In this case, however, much of the content will consist of derivative pieces that will benefit from the quality of the sources from which they are derived.

Consolidation must be done at the channel level, as well. Going back to Exercise 4, let's revisit the inventory of channels with our content grid at hand. Now, you're looking for insights about which content types align with which channels. Here's a sample line of inquiry to help you identify consolidation opportunities:

- Do you have two or more channels that address similar personas at similar stages?
  - If yes, does one have significantly more reach than the others?
    - If so, consider consolidating to aggregate your audience and increase the critical mass of the channel with greater reach. This will also reduce channel overhead and simplify your content development process.
  - If no, maintain existing channels.
- Does each channel have at least one unique content type that cannot be found elsewhere?

This second question points to a general principle of content strategy: namely, that each channel and each content type has unique affordances and opportunities associated with it. By organizing and sequencing content delivery by channel and content type, it's possible to encourage individuals to move further down the funnel. For example, owned channels are typically more effective at the bottom of the funnel because you have the most control of the experience with owned channels. Consequently, restricting your most valuable content to your owned properties can be an effective means of driving people down the funnel. Content at the top of the funnel tends to be more granular, shorter in form, and pithy, whereas content gets more narrative, in-depth, and insightful as you move down the funnel.

Many companies have a tendency to distribute all content via all channels ("I invested in this content, darn it; I want to reap its full reward!"). This is generally not a smart approach, however, because channels become less differentiated and less effective for specific personas—and they generally become cluttered. Plus, you limit your ability to give a potential customer a reason to opt into a new channel that may have greater affordances for engagement. (See Chapter 3, where I talk about the importance of setting up a fair value exchange with the customer at each stage of their journey.) If the customer wants your most valuable content, he should be willing to provide something in return, such as an opt-in or a piece of data.

Agile Content Strategy in Practice

The previous exercise is an ideal setup for a conversation about your overall content strategy practice, because it forces content marketers to think about which channels are best for which personas and content types. But you must supplement the insights derived from the eight preceding exercises with traditional research to fully understand how content consumption is evolving and how it will affect your business.

Your content strategy will thus emerge from the prioritization of your content backlogs and your analysis of content channels. The stakeholders for this discussion will be your editorial board, including representatives from product management and other leadership functions, all of whom require content support. (Refer to the strategy exercises described in Chapter 12, but instead of applying them to your overall marketing initiatives, apply them to your content initiatives—those items in your content marketing backlog.)

However, as I explain in Chapter 12, these insights must be reconciled with the day-to-day feedback that emerges from the Agile content team that is actively iterating on your content—and from the automated programs, websites, and services that deliver content. This raises an issue that many marketers struggle with today: namely, how to measure the performance of their content. Most marketers have some relevant technologies in place that can support day-to-day iteration, such as web analytics for measuring content sharing and content performance.

What's less common is a solution for aggregating data in ways that support the content strategy framework that I've laid out in this chapter. Today, many marketers use shared spreadsheets or wikis to capture data snapshots for the content marketing exercises. Unfortunately, as the company develops a full portfolio of content, this can quickly become unwieldy. For this reason, technologies that support content marketing have been a focus area of investment and innovation. At Oracle, for instance, we have a content marketing solution that supports content planning, workflow, publishing, and analytics. In general, such technologies provide workflows that structure how source content is created and sliced and diced into derivative content. They also organize content in the ways I've outlined, making it possible to easily sort content types by persona, stage, formality, and so forth. And this, in turn, supports the analysis outlined in Exercise 8.

The content marketing framework approaches your content as if it were a product. It compels marketers to iterate on content over time to improve its performance while optimizing their overall portfolios. In addition, it effectively establishes a service that any stakeholder can use to find the right content to support the customer's digital body language. And this service will help them evaluate the quality and performance of such content virtually in real time.

Combining this content marketing framework with a marketing automation service makes it possible to optimize the content consumption patterns that support your overall customer experience. Your automation platform will leverage the data associated with how prospects and customers engage with content—and content programs—to form a picture of their digital body language. Going back to the book's conclusion, this is the kind of data that adds value to the customer experience database and that informs topic scores for individuals and companies. So when marketers look at the customer life cycle holistically, it's now possible to use the insights that emerge from the content marketing framework to improve customer experience across the entire life cycle.

Appendix 2:
The Product Manager's Perspective on Agile Marketing

My aim with *The Agile Marketer* is to make the case that marketing, product development, and product management must work in concert to create a better product and an enhanced customer experience—and in doing so, achieve competitive advantage. And while the preponderance of my research involved interviews and conversations with marketers, many of the ideas and examples in this book also (necessarily) came from the product development and management sides. Because these sides represent marketing's primary business partner in the modern marketing context, it seemed appropriate to provide readers more firsthand perspectives from seasoned product practitioners.

To that end, I interviewed three accomplished product developers/managers whose individual experience gives them important personal and even historical perspective on these questions. Each has used Agile in a wide range of product development contexts and throughout their careers, and all have strong feelings about the promise of the marketing/product partnership.

Kenneth Berger is a veteran product manager and advisor/investor. He was the first product manager at Slack, the office messaging application start-up founded in 2014. Berger helped the company (creator of one of the fastest-growing business apps in history) grow tenfold, from 100,000 to more than 1 million daily active users. Previously, he co-founded YesGraph, another enterprise start-up backed by Andreessen Horowitz and Accel. At Adobe, he helped build some of the company's first software-as-a-service products, managed the $100 million-plus Dreamweaver business, and drove critical acquisitions including Typekit, Omniture, and Behance.

Clara Liang is chief product officer at Jive, the communications and collaborative software company, where she is responsible for the vision, design, and delivery of the company's products. Liang has more than 15 years of experience building enterprise-grade products and a background that spans product design and engineering as well as the delivery of technical services. Previously, Liang held a number of senior positions at IBM where she led product management and engineering for Cast Iron Systems; served as chief of staff to the VP of WebSphere; and oversaw product management for Emerging Technologies and Cloud. Liang has also held positions at Yahoo!, Roche, and the Carnegie Institute of Washington.

Neil Lamka has more than 40 years of experience in the data processing industry, in a wide range of industries and roles. He has been a systems programmer, data center operations manager, systems engineering manager, developer, chief architect, technology strategist, and product manager. Lamka has served as a product manager or product executive at small start-ups (such as LiveCapital and HomeGain.com), mid-sized companies (such as ServiceSource International), and large multinationals (such as Dun & Bradstreet) and has consulted to E*Trade Securities and VISA International. He began his career at IBM, where he spent 16 years in a variety of technical and management positions. Lamka currently consults on new product definition and product development-level process re-engineering.

I spoke with each of these experts about Agile's benefits and limitations, its influence on marketing, and the evolving relationship between product management and marketing. Herewith are excerpts from our conversations.

Roland Smart: Increasingly, we're seeing technology procurement and technology management shifting from a centralized place and directly into the lines of business. This trend is affecting the chief marketing officer more profoundly than any other C-suite role. This is primarily what is driving marketers' interest in Agile—and their willingness to be influenced by the development and product management teams that are conversant in Agile.

At the same time, product management and its leaders are gaining unprecedented power and influence. In this book I argue that marketers will gain influence with product management if they embrace Agile because Agile fosters mutual understanding and closer collaboration. It's the glue that creates this new partnership. How do you see marketing and product management collaborating? And what role do you think Agile plays?

Kenneth Berger: I've definitely seen marketing move closer to product management. In the teams I have worked on, collaborating on development has been really effective in making marketing not feel like a whole separate department that stands for something entirely different. My takeaway is that in some ways, Agile as a process can be a lingua franca for product development in working with product management. That is certainly the way it started out. But I think it's also a language for product management to work with marketing, and for marketing to work directly with development.

The whole point of having this Agile process is not just to have a better structure for your own work, but to be able to work with other people. Working with other people doesn't just mean learning some process from a book; it means actually collaborating effectively with them. And that means being flexible about the processes that people agree on. It means understanding that we all have limited resources so we need to prioritize. To me, if this way of working is the future of marketing and product management, that's a very bright future.

Clara Liang: I think there's a newer style of leadership that's needed today in order to adapt and be agile and innovate. How can we be strong together? How do we actually team together to get the right outcome for the business? Leadership teams must behave more collaboratively than ever before. I think it's actually a requirement today, to compete and to succeed.

Great CIOs, those who are going to lead their companies to success, want to partner with great line-of-business leaders. You're seeing that same dynamic between marketing and product today. If you want to build the most innovative, agile, fit-for-market, and fit-for-user product, your marketers and your product team have to be connected at the hip like never before. Your long-term vision—your North Star—is a multiyear vision. Your Agile releases, if you will, or iterations, those are just turns of the crank that help you progress toward that vision. Agile is a must, because it's the only way you can continue to innovate. When you can be more connected up front, more collaborative, more responsive in building those tactical iterations, that serves the end goal.

You can only do that when you're truly partnered up cross-functionally and when you're focused on the end-goal serving the user with the most relevant product possible.

Berger: During my time at Adobe, the company really wanted to adopt the most modern processes, so it instituted formal Scrum training, not just for development or product management, but also for some marketing people. There was some sense that Agile was going to be the new lingua franca—a new process to bring all these people together. That if everyone had thought they understood the process before, now they were *really* going to need to understand this new thing if they wanted to be able to collaborate. To me, that's the reason that Agile processes are so important. They give people a level playing ground on which to work together, instead of people pursuing their work in isolation, thinking, "Oh well, development decides on the architecture, and product decides on features, and marketing works on distribution channels," when increasingly those things are interrelated.

At the start-ups I've worked at, it wasn't about new processes for the sake of being new ("Oh, we need to get on this latest process"). Instead, we had a sense that our whole competitive advantage was about being state-of-the-art—about not being constrained by established processes or convention. So we were always, by default, working with state-of-the-art systems and processes of all kinds. Adobe was the sort of company that recognized that, on the one hand, there were a lot of valuable things to protect in terms of the existing businesses and the processes and systems that produced them. But on the other hand, we could see the handwriting on the wall The traditional shipping process at Adobe used to be every two years, then it became every 18 months, and then it became every year. The company correctly saw that the shrinking of the cycle was a big accomplishment but realized that it was still very, very far from being state-of-the-art when everyone else was already doing continuous deployment and pushing new versions out to the web every few hours. So Adobe recognized that it needed to make a big change, and investing in Agile training was the way to do it.

I think Adobe's story is a really hopeful one. It's easy to get great process stories from start-ups that don't have the kind of constraints that big companies have. Adobe was able to move from being a pretty traditionally oriented company to being SaaS-based, doing much faster turnarounds, having Scrum and Agile be a part of the vocabulary for a large portion of the company. That's not easy. And it took a long time. But they still did it. But I think it only started paying out its full value when the business model was aligned. Because if the business model is not aligned, you don't really have an incentive to fully buy in to new processes. Okay, you might be re-prioritizing and listening to customers in a different way, but if you're not delivering on that value in real time, who can actually tell? What difference are you making to the customer?

Smart: As I discuss in the book, Agile has its limitations. Marketing and product management leaders must supplement Agile with strategic practices. From the standpoint of a strict interpretation of the Agile Manifesto, the Agile approach is often seen as being inconsistent with planning because it's based on feedback on the now instead of on a longer horizon and longer term vision. I argue that strategic planning may not fit into your Agile practice but that it can still be integrated with it. Tell me: How have your respective teams reconciled their Agile practices with their strategic ones?

Liang: Here's how I think about it: that vision, that strategic goal—that North Star—that's your guiding principle. It's critical for a company to have one, and your leadership team has to be clear about it and aligned on it. You also have business goals, set annually, quarterly, or as appropriate for your context. The vision and goals must be completely cascaded through the company. That's what creates the ability for teams, for your Agile teams, and even for individual contributors to be able to act with some degree of autonomy. When they know the North Star and the goals, individual teams can build their plans. It's especially important for companies at scale, like an IBM or an Oracle; how else do you make sure the individual is always building their iterations in alignment with the strategy? They have to know what the North Star is and are completely empowered to move that way. That's how you get to speed, and that's how you get execution at scale.

Within each iteration, you tie back to the vision and goals. You develop hypotheses and look to prove them "By focusing on feature X or Y in this iteration, we will positively impact goals A and B, which serve our priorities and vision." You then evaluate the results of each iteration to determine whether or not you're making progress.

For me, it's about an individual having clarity about the North Star and business goals so that they can build meaningful, iterative plans and you can evaluate if you're making proper progress toward your hypotheses. If you're not, that's where you need to adjust. It doesn't mean you have to adjust your North Star. It could mean that you just need to adjust some of your tactics.

Berger: At Slack, we had a very real-time, reactive practice at all levels of the company, where we were reacting in a typically Agile way to individual development hiccups. But we weren't only looking at that. We were also always looking at the high-level road map. I was meeting with leadership every few weeks to make sure that we still thought that all these given features should be done in this particular order—and what about all these other new variables that came up? We were able to react quickly to feedback, or at least have the conversation, on an ongoing basis at multiple levels—at the most basic level, even at the piece-of-the-feature level with the design team, as well as at the very highest level of the company. At all levels we asked: What features should we do and when? What's our major emphasis for this quarter or this year?

We thought of this less as a process to follow and more as a discipline that we had. We weren't going to make a plan and then never look at it again. We were going to make all sorts of plans in different areas of the company for each person's job, but we were also going to recognize that those plans would all change. That's a big part of Agile right there.

Smart: Neil, in recent years you've had considerable experience in industries outside of tech, like financial services. How do you see the reconciliation between Agile and strategy practices?

Lamka: The differences I see have more to do with how things are actually practiced in more established companies day to day versus what happens in Silicon Valley. The fact is, the tech sector drives what's new, and some practices haven't yet made their way into mainstream practice.

In my view, one of product management's roles is to provide a framework in which implementation choices can be made, and I think part of marketing's role is to provide a framework in which innovation can occur. So this idea is to have a road map, have some big blocks of capability that show directionally where you jointly want the product to go, what is the position of the product going forward over the next 18 months or two years. But with the understanding that they're big blocks of capability and it's only directionally correct. From day to day, none of that is going to happen on that schedule by itself. It's really a communications and cooperation thing between marketing and product—and one that in my experience doesn't really happen that much today. But it needs to happen.

Part of my job is to bridge the customer to engineering or development, and to bridge marketing to engineering and development, and to establish a process, a means of regular communication in both directions between those organizations. Right now, the things going to market that *should* be more agile, are always at the end. Basically, marketing and product management don't start collaborating until late in the process, when the product is ready to ship. So as the product management person, what do I do now? I've got stuff that's supposed to be delivered in the next two weeks. And what does marketing do to reconcile, particularly in a fast-paced business? What's a big enough increment of change to actually talk about? If every time I changed something I communicated it on the website, then the visitor would quickly become numb to that kind of change. So what's the right cadence for marketing and product development for [*bona fide*] product announcements and releases, versus minor releases or defect-fixing kinds of releases? That's a conversation that we don't have very often today. If you had established triggers for marketing releases, a regular cadence for them, then you'd have an excuse to have more regularly scheduled discussions between product and marketing.

Similarly, if you had a joint road map and regularly scheduled reviews of where you are on the road map, what adjustments need to be made, and what you are learning between product and marketing and engineering, In other words, engineering makes contributions about what is possible, marketing makes contributions about what is needed or useful or desired by customers, and product management figures out how it fits on the road map and how best to sequence what is built and what is released. If this happens than I think you'd get to the point where you could demonstrate value, just like adoption of Agile in the first place.

Smart: I see many opportunities for marketing and product management to collaborate on research. In your work, where do you see this happening—and where are there are opportunities for improvement?

Liang: At Jive, the product marketer and product manager are almost one. It's as though they share part of their brains, and the other half extends into their own respective domain. So the product marketing organization is very connected to the brand strategy, the marketing strategy, how analysts' think about the product, their relationships with the press, and macro trends. It's also connected to market opportunity, market dynamics, and buyer issues: their pain points, use cases, user research, et cetera. The buyer issues are where the product marketer and product manager share the brain. Product management has to understand who the buyer is: What's their profile? What's their pain? I don't think that it's a, "Hey, let's-just-sit-down-and-have-a-meeting-about-it" type relationship with marketing. I think that's where there is—or must be—genuine overlap.

Over the past year, Jive has been transforming to become much more product- and market-centric. And one of the things that we've seen work really well is early concept buyer studies. The product manager and the product marketer observe those together. They comb through the transcripts together. They actually ask those questions together and then they have a dialogue about what each of them took from it. And then they explore how that comes together in terms of something we would want to do. When product manager and product marketer partner together in that process, it helps the product manager be much more connected in building the requirements and articulating to design and engineering what we're about to build. I think the more interlock you can have, the better.

We've also seen success with design and engineering's participation in the studies when they (or a couple of the engineers) take part in the studies, and also get a readout of the study results. That's what gives you that holistic context. So when you start going into the planning, design, and implementation phases, you have real, tangible end users and buyers front and center in your mind. The old hand-off used to be tossing it over the wall. "Hey, I have this data. I'm going to throw it over the wall to product management." Then product management says, "Here's what's in the release" and throws it back over the wall. For some types of products, that was still very common even just five years ago. Agile is in service of innovating more quickly and allowing you to adjust and stay more relevant, so you don't run yourself off a cliff. Agile helps you avoid this with cross-functional teams.

Lamka: in my experience in the product organization, there isn't—or hasn't been—a whole lot of conversation or input from marketing, in terms of instrumenting the product for gathering what marketing would consider meaningful marketing data.

What I've seen is that you might get interesting information by happenstance, or by doing minor things to get relevant information. For example, adding simple Google Analytics tags to various web pages provides some information that may be useful. Actually thinking about the problem in terms of defining marketing-specific information-gathering requirements and building them into the product would be much more impactful and informative, though. But there hasn't yet really been a big movement toward requirement feeds or any discussion about what would be useful in terms of instrumenting the products for gathering marketing information. And with the focus now on trying to get actionable information from the customer's experience, that is something that we'll be seeing more of. There'll be more pressure on the product side to incorporate those kinds of things, and not just the pure customer-facing features. Not only more of the rapid prototyping and prototype-sharing with customers through a marketing/product cooperative face to the customer, but also actually doing A/B testing and the like within the product itself—the baked-in marketing, as you like to call it. And then quickly capturing metrics and measurements out of that and then being able to take action. It's a form of direct marketing involvement that influences the product.

Berger: I'm biased, because I come from the world of user research, so I'm very much a proponent of research at all times. But in my view, research is a competency that any number of groups across a company should be well versed in. And which ones are doing what kind of research is tied to your context. With sales, for instance, you think of them as leads. So even if it's very early stage and they're not necessarily qualified yet, you want to be starting to build a relationship. So you're going to have a certain type of research feedback in place because you really do care about meeting the needs of this individual customer. At a product management or marketing level, on the other hand, maybe you're thinking much more about it in aggregate. You don't necessarily care about the feedback of any individual customer, but you want to get a broader sense of your customer segments, your most interesting areas for research, or the personas that you want to focus on.

I'm agnostic about who should do that work, as long as it's done and as long as the people are aligned. Because I think that some of the most valuable marketing research that we did at Slack was really research that people across functions all participated in. It was around on-boarding and user experience, and that is one of the most naturally interdisciplinary pieces of the product you could work on. Engineering definitely cares about it, product management definitely cares about it, marketing cares, sales cares—and they all have something real to contribute to the process to make sure that their piece of the puzzle is filled in. And the research was successful in part because it wasn't wholly owned by any one of those groups. All of the groups had different things to take away from it, but we were very much unified around a single goal "This is what we need to do for the customer, so we know now we can divide and conquer according to our context." I agree that research is generally too siloed. Oftentimes, the marketing team is working on the quarterly customer satisfaction survey, and the product managers are looking at their analytics dashboard. To me, the problem is not that the product people need the expertise of marketers; it's more that everyone is looking at what they're doing too narrowly. Just because the customer satisfaction survey is something that the marketing groups are more skilled at or most familiar with or that's most valuable doesn't mean that they can't get secondary value out of the analytics, or that there isn't a third area beyond surveys and analytics that both parties could get a lot of information from. So, to me, I think about research as being less discipline-based and more goal-based.

Smart: Some business leaders claim (rather vocally) that they hate marketing. Even creative, cutting-edge entrepreneurs like Ben Chestnut of MailChimp—someone who actually embeds marketing in everything he does—say they hate it. But I contend that when they say that, they're not thinking of Agile marketing; they're thinking of the traditional approach to marketing. So the problem is that inspirational product leaders are more apt to talk about their dissatisfaction with the traditional approach than they are to acknowledge that there is a new approach that is working well for them. What's your experience with this, and do you see it changing?

Berger: Well, I'm an odd person to ask because my first role as a product manager was with the same team that I had been working before in user research. I switched roles because I realized that I could move into product management and still do user research, but I would have a lot more influence in other areas of the product. I'd be better able to have a holistic understanding and a holistic influence on the direction of the product line. I think to some degree that's true of any role, right? There's always the small vision of what you're tasked to do, the bare minimum of what your job is. Whether it's just buying ads or writing or creating messaging, or on the product management side, just writing specs and assigning work to engineers. Then we all have a bigger vision of our role and what it *can* be. And to me, that comes down to the team leaders and their individual team members being willing and able to step up in a meaningful way.

What's happening now is that people are recognizing how complex and important marketing really is, and because it is so complex and important, it's becoming more central to the enterprise. That means different things to different (internal) organizations. It could mean that product management starts absorbing more of these marketing-related processes. Or it could happen the way it happened at Slack, where the chief marketing officer, Bill Macaitis, has not just all of marketing underneath him, but also all of sales. He is very, very influential in the company. That said, I think you're right that most marketers are in a kind of traditional role. I think you're right that product management has generally moved into a more central, and more powerful, role. But I don't think that what's stopping marketers from making a difference is the perception about marketing. That's always a barrier, but you could say that of any role. Everyone is expected to do something that's pretty narrow, and the only way to break out of it is to break out of it. I think you're right about the overall trends, but what makes me optimistic about the role of marketing in the future is thinking about those individual marketers that I've worked with. They haven't been worried about what marketing traditionally is. They've just worked with all the people around them to get stuff done.

Lamka: In many cases, weak marketing organizations—and the accompanying lack of perceived value—tend to get discounted. [For product management] it's not worth the time to try to cultivate those relationships, because the return on investment is either nonexistent or extremely low. Because of the power shift that you outlined, Roland, the marketing organization needs to be more aggressive in two respects: one, injecting themselves into the process, and two, understanding how they can actually provide value. Part of that value is going away for six months to do a market research study of some kind that can be helpful. Your marketing group might be looking at long-term marketing trends, which is fine. But those people need a way to interact with product management on shorter term deliverables in order to demonstrate value. Unless there's some continuous feedback that says, "We're projecting that the market will go into this specific area, or that our next tranche of customers will come from this segment and they'll have some unique capability needs," all assumptions will have to be tested and validated because it is all unknown. After all, if we could see the future, we'd all be rich and retired. But we're looking at these trends, we think there are these gaps, we think there are these risks. I think that identifying these things is a marketing organization role—they're much better at that than product people are. And when product people think they can do that better, you're in trouble. Because that's not where we have either the skills or (in most cases) the interest. And if it's not interesting, you're not going to do it well. But unless marketing can be responsive, unless they can be collaborative, and unless they can be agile (not to overuse the term)—unless they can actually handle requests and participate, then they will continue to be marginalized, particularly in organizations where they think all you need is a good idea.

Liang: I would say the best product leaders that I interact with absolutely recognize that not only is the product management style evolving, but so is the marketing style. If you go back, say 10 years, product management looked more like program management or like executing a set of tasks that were decided by a different team, whether by an executive staff, or marketing, or engineering, or some other group. As product has evolved to have more of a balance between the tactical and the strategic in building an integrated plan that serves the company vision, that same trend is happening in marketing. We talk a lot about building amazing and relevant products and that the best products can be amazing marketing, maybe even your best marketing. But unless you're totally lucky, you only get that best amazing relevant product when you've done market research, when you have that context, when you have studied your data and your users in the market trends and done the analysis to know how to continue to build and serve that vision in the best way possible.

That's where that real magic partnership comes between product management and product marketing, getting you to the right product. Once you have the right product, adding brand or corporate marketing is your amplifier. That creates your halo, it creates demand, and then it helps drive user acquisition. So if you haven't had the privilege of working with a great marketing partner who's also undergoing this transformation, then it's very easy to paint marketing into a corner—just like it's easy to paint engineering or design, or product management into a corner that says, "They just build the stuff." You recognize that all of us have to have a higher level of consciousness that our collaborative input and collective thinking make for a better product. That's where I think you really get magic, and it's hard and rare to find all of the components, all of the team members that actually think that way.

Let's take an example from B2B software. The buyer journey today is changing and more complicated than ever before. Buyers research online, start free trials, and read user feedback often before engaging in a sales conversation—if there is one at all. Often, products are even purchased online without ever talking to a salesperson. In this world, the entire journey is one connected process. There is no clear hand off of the user between product and marketing. It's about a whole product experience for your end user or your customer The leading marketers are making that shift, just like the product leaders are, just like engineering leaders are, just like design leaders are. So that what we show on the website and what you see when you are actually in the product, really feel like they're reflective of one brand, one visual language, one experience. All those connections need to be there. We've been talking a lot about marketing and product, but this applies just as much to design and marketing, to marketing and engineering, to engineering and product, engineering and design. All of those connections have to be really tight. It's really that collaborative in nature.

Agile just becomes the framework that encourages you to have those conversations. And it gives you some structure for moving this way. But above all, it really is a competitive imperative that you think and function this way. I think there is a tremendous opportunity for improvement because organizational silos tend to create natural divides in communication. What we're really talking about here, and why you and I sit on two sides of the same problem, is that modern leaders need to think beyond their organizational structure and work beyond what is natural in that structure. That's where the Agile team, and the focus on the goal brings a cross-functional team together. It gives them something to unite around toward that North Star.

Resources

- Blogs
  - The Agile Marketing Blog www.agilemarketingblog.com
  - Jim Ewel's Agile Marketing Blog www.agilemarketing.net/marketing-agile
  - Scott Brinner's Cheifmartec Blog http://chiefmartec.com
- Podcasts
  - The Marketing Agility Podcast https://itunes.apple.com/us/podcast/marketing-agility-podcast/id410175356
- References Documents
  - Henrik Kniberg's and Mattias Skarin's publication entitled Kanban and Scrum, making the most of both www.google.com/search?q=%E2%80%A2%09Henrik+Kniberg+%26+Mattias+Skarin%E2%80%99s+publication+entitled+Kanban+and+Scrum%2C+making+the+most+of+both&ie=utf-8&oe=utf-8.
  - The Agile Marketing Manifesto http://agilemarketingmanifesto.org
- Jonathan Rasmusson's Agile in a Nutshell www.agilenutshell.com
  - Agile Marketing Resource—A Compendium for Marketing Agility
  - http://agilemarketingresource.com
  - The Agile Alliance http://guide.agilealliance.org
- Community
  - Join an Agile Marketing Meetup, www.meetup.com
  - Join the Topliners Marketing Community, https://community.oracle.com/community/topliners
  - Join the Growthhacker Community https://growthhackers.com/
- Books
  - *A New Brand of Marketing*, Scott Brinker, Boston Massachusetts, 2014
  - *Growing Up Fast: How New Agile Practices Can Move Marketing and Innovation Past the Old Business Stalemates*

- Jascha Kaykas-Wolff (Author), Kevin Fann (Author), Sean Martinez (Illustrator), *Marketing Iteration, 2014,*
- *The Lean Startup: How Today's Entrepreneurs Use Continuous Innovation to Create Radically Successful Businesses*, Eric Ries, Crown Business, 2011.
- Agile Tools
  - Asana, https://asana.com
  - Pivotaltracker, www.pivotaltracker.com
  - Jira, www.atlassian.com/software/jira
  - LeanKit, http://leankit.com
  - KanbanTool, http://kanbantool.com
  - VersionOne, www.versionone.com

Endnotes

Chapter 1 Why Marketing Needs to Adapt

1. Tesla Motors forums/community website, "TESLA WANTS FEEDBACK ON ANY POOR (OR GREAT!) CUSTOMER EXPERIENCES," Nick Howe, November 7, 2012, http://my.teslamotors.com/forum/forums/tesla-wants-feedback-any-poor-or-great-customer-experiences.
2. Gartner website, Jake Sorofman and Laura McLellan, "Gartner Survey Finds Importance of Customer Experience on the Rise—Marketing Is on the Hook," https://www.gartner.com/doc/2857722/gartner-survey-finds-importance-customer.

Chapter 2 The Modern Marketer's Challenge

1. Peter Drucker, "Innovation and Entrepreneurship." *HarperBusiness*, reprint 2006.
2. Lars Backstrom and Jon Kleinberg, "Romantic Partnerships and the Dispersion of Social Ties: A Network Analysis of Relationship Status on Facebook," Proceedings from the 17th Conference on Computer-Supported Cooperative Work and Social Computing, February 2014, http://arxiv.org/pdf/1310.6753v1.pdf.
3. Elon Musk, Tesla Motors Blog, "All Our Patent Are Belong To You," June 12, 2014, www.teslamotors.com/blog/all-our-patent-are-belong-you.

Chapter 3 Scaling Sales: Marketing and the Role of Automation

1. Peter Drucker, "Management: Tasks, Responsibilities, Practices," *HarperBusiness*, 1973.

2. Marketing Leadership Council, MLC Customer Purchase Research Survey," Corporate Executive Board, 2011, www.google.com/search? q=MLC+Customer+Purchase+Research+Survey&ie=utf-8&oe=utf-8.

3. "Calculating The Real ROI from Lead Nurturing." *DemandGen Report*, April 22, 2009.

4. Jim Ewel, "What is Agile Marketing?," Agile Marketing website, 2014, www.agilemarketing.net/what-is-agile-marketing.

5. Steve Jobs Interview, http://openvault.wgbh.org/catalog/7b7ae3-steve-jobs-interview, WGBH Open Vault, May 14, 1990. Steve Jobs recounted a story—on many occasions—about reading a *Scientific American* article that compared the speed of animals under their own power. The human was far from the top of the list. When they included a human on a bicycle, however, the human far surpassed the fastest animal. Jobs then stated that he viewed the computer as the bicycle of the mind.

6. "May 2013 Occupational Employment Statistics," United States Bureau of Labor Statistics, May 2014, www.google.com/search?q=May+2013+Occupational+Employment+Statistics&ie=utf-8&oe=utf-8.

7. Christine Moorman, "From Marketing Spend to Marketing Accountability," *Marketing News*, The CMO Survey, May 2014, http://cmosurvey.org/files/2014/06/From-Marketing-Spend-to-Marketing-Accountability.pdf.

Chapter 4 The Rise of Agile

1. This quote is generally attributed to Charles Darwin but there is some debate regarding its provenance. This exact quote is more likely to be

from another scholar paraphrasing (evolving?) content from Darwin's journals. http://quoteinvestigator.com/2014/05/04/adapt/.

2. Kent Beck, Mike Beedle, Arie van Bennekum, Alistair Cockburn, Ward Cunningham, Martin Fowler, James Grenning, Jim Highsmith, Andrew Hunt, Ron Jeffries, Jon Kern, Brian Marick, Robert C. Martin, Steve Mellor, Ken Schwaber, Jeff Sutherland, and Dave Thomas, "The Agile Manifesto," February 13, 2001, http://agilemanifesto.org/

3. Google Trends, "Agile Marketing vs. Inbound Marketing," August 2015, https://www.google.com/trends/explore#q=Agile%20Marketing%2C %20Inbound%20Marketing&cmpt=q&tz=Etc%2FGMT%2B7.

Chapter 6 The Skinny on Scrum

1. Jonathan Rasmusson, "Three Simple Truths," Agile in a Nutshell, 2015, www.agilenutshell.com/three_simple_truths.

Chapter 7 Kanban: Lean Meets Agile

1. Henrik Kniberg and Mattias Skarin, "Kanban vs. Scrum: Making the Most of Both," *InfoQ*, 2010.

Chapter 8 Implementing Agile: Key Considerations

1. Peter High, "For J.Crew's CIO, Slow and Steady Wins the Race in the First 100 Days," *Forbes*, October 17, 2013, www.forbes.com/sites/peterhigh/ 2013/10/07/for-j-crews-cio-slow-and-steady-wins-the-race-in-the-first- 100-days/.

2. Defense.gov News Transcript, "DoD News Briefing—Secretary Rumsfeld and Gen. Myers, United States Department of Defense," www.defense .gov.

Chapter 9 Implementing Agile: Common Objections

1. www.agilenutshell.com/three_simple_truths
2. Laura Ramos, "B2B CMOs Must Evolve or Move On," Forrester Research, July 23, 2013, http://solutions.forrester.com/Global/FileLib/ Reports/B2B_CMOs_Must_Evolve_Or_Move_On.pdf.
3. Bjarte Bogsnes, "The World Has Changed—Isn't It Time to Change the Way We Lead and Manage?" Harvard Business Publishing, June 2010, Vol. 12 No. 3, https://hbr.org/product/the-world-has-changed-isn-t-it-time-to-change-the-way-we-lead-and-manage/B1005A-PDF-ENG.
4. Bjarte Bogsnes, "Dynamic Forecasting: A Planning Innovation for Fast-Changing Times," *Balanced Scorecard Report*, Harvard Business Publishing, September 2009, www.capitols.ru/d/414335/d/wp-hbr-dynamic-forecasting-a-planning-innovation.pdf.

Chapter 10 Your North Star: The Agile Marketing Manifesto

1. The Agile Marketing Manifesto, http://agilemarketingmanifesto.org/.
2. Eric Ries. "Minimum Viable Product: A Guide," August 3, 2009, www .startuplessonslearned.com/2009/08/minimum-viable-product-guide .html.

Chapter 12 Beyond Agile: More Methods to Link Marketing and Product Management with Innovation

1. Peter Drucker, "The Practice of Management," *HarperBusiness*, 1954.
2. Sherryl Patek, David Cooperstein, and Alexandra Hayes, "Quick Take: Three Ways That the Right CMO-CIO Partnership Can Pack a Powerful Punch," *Forrester Research*, November 13, 2013.
3. Ibid.

4. Adaptive Path Blog, "Setting Priorities," April 24, 2002, www .adaptivepath.com/ideas/e000018.
5. Patek, Cooperstein, and Hayes, "Quick Take."

Chapter 13 Beyond Agile: Marketing's Role in the Customer Experience

1. Jake Sorofman, "Customer Experience Emerges as the Marketers' Next Battlefield," Gartner, October, 24, 2014, http://blogs.gartner.com/ jake-sorofman/gartner-surveys-confirm-customer-experience-new-battlefield/.
2. Wikipedia, Gestalt Psychology, http://en.wikipedia.org/wiki/Gestalt_ psychology.
3. Edward Tufte, "Envisioning Information," Graphics Press, 1990.
4. "The Insurer: Delivering Exceptional Customer Experiences," Accenture, August 2013, http://insuranceblog.accenture.com/wp-content/ uploads/2013/09/Accenture-12459660-Delivering-Exceptional-Experiences.pdf.
5. Karen Freeman, Patrick Spenner, and Anna Bird, "Three Myths about What Customers Want," *Harvard Business Review,* May 23, 2012, https:// hbr.org/2012/05/three-myths-about-customer-eng.
6. "2014 B2B Buyer Behavior Survey," *DemandGen Report,* January 29, 2014, www.demandgenreport.com/industry-resources/research/2508-the-2014-b2b-buyer-behavior-survey.html.
7. Katrina Bradley and Richard Hatherall, "Mastering the Episodes That Count with Customers," *Bain Brief,* June 30, 2015, www.bain.com/ publications/articles/mastering-the-episodes-that-count-with-customers .aspx.

Chapter 15: Growth Hacking

1. Lauren Hockenson, "Growth Hacker: A Buzzword Surrounded by Buzzwords,"*Mashable*, May 18, 2013, http://mashable.com/2013/05/18/ growth-hacker-buzzwords/.

2. The Agile Marketing Meetup San Francisco, https://growthhackers .com/slides/agile-marketing-meetup-moving-beyond-the-marketing-plan-so-you-remaiGrowthhacking.com. In addition to this presentation you can find a detailed case study, "High Tempo Testing Revives GrowthHackers.com Growth" at http://growthhackers.com/growth-studies/high-tempo-testing-revives-growthhackers-com-growth.

3. Rebecca Lieb, "The Converged Media Imperative: How Brands Must Combine Paid, Owned & Earned Media," Altimeter Group, July 19, 2012, www.altimetergroup.com/2012/07/the-converged-media-imperative/.

4. Edelman TrustBarometer, www.edelman.com/2015-edelman-trust-barometer/.

5. "Talking to Strangers: Millennials Trust People Over Brands." *Bazaar-Voice,* January 2012, http://resources.bazaarvoice.com/rs/bazaarvoice/images/201202_Millennials_whitepaper.pdf.

Chapter 16: Lessons from the Collaborative Economy

1. It's worth taking a moment to compare the previous versions of the infographic. All are available online, along with the blog posts in which Owyang shares the changes and updates that have contributed to making this infographic a veritable reference document. www.web-strategist.com/blog/2014/12/07/collaborative-economy-honeycomb-2-watch-it-grow/.

2. Georgios Zervas, Davide Proserpio, John W. Byers, "The Rise of the Shar-ing Economy: Estimating the Impact of Airbnb on the Hotel Industry," Boston University, May 7, 2015, http://people.bu.edu/zg/publications/airbnb.pdf.

3. "The Sharing Economy—Sizing the Revenue Opportunity," Pricewa-terhouseCoopers, 2015, www.pwc.co.uk/issues/megatrends/collisions/sharingeconomy/the-sharing-economy-sizing-the-revenue-opportunity .html.

Conclusion: The Steward of Customer Experience

1. Charles Duhigg, "How Companies Learn Your Secrets," *New York Times*, February 16, 2012, www.nytimes.com/2012/02/19/magazine/shopping-habits.html.

About the Author

Roland Smart believes that marketing is going through a transformation driven by new technologies and practices. He is a proponent of integrating Agile—the approach that revolutionized software development—with marketing. Doing so positions the chief marketing officer alongside the chief product officer as the two primary drivers of the business. This, in turn, enables the chief marketing officer to serve as the steward of the overall customer experience—not just the brand—at a time when companies are increasingly competing on this basis.

Roland is a product-oriented marketing leader who serves as the VP of social and community marketing at Oracle. As such, he oversees Oracle's user communities and advocacy program. He also manages acquired marketing technologies (e.g., Compendium) for the corporate marketing group. Roland joined Oracle through its acquisition of Involver, a social technology platform. Before that, he led the marketing team at Sprout, a social/mobile ad creation platform (acquired by InMobi). Roland developed a passion for product development, user experience, and agile practices while running the marketing team at Adaptive Path, a leading San Francisco–based user experience design firm (acquired by CapitalOne).

Roland lives with his wife and son in Marin, California, where he can often be found hiking and mountain biking in Golden Gate National Recreation Area.

Index

Note: Page references in *italics* refer to figures.